Have
You
Ever....?

Have You Ever...?

Thoughts on God
from the Carpool Line

MARGARET CHAMBERS YOUNG

This book is lovingly and with great thanksgiving
dedicated to those people in my life who played the
largest roles in helping me to understand what it means to
be a child of God:
to my parents, Wicke and Rufus Chambers,
and my husband's parents, Jane and Bill Young,
who raised both of us with the Christlike love God
desired for them to give;
to my husband, Bill, who has blessed me with
the best family a girl could ever dream to have;
to my children, Billy and Brandon, who have taught me
the real lessons of what it means to be a child;
and to God Himself, for opening my eyes to His love
and gift as my perfect heavenly Father.

Published by
Looking Glass Books
730 Sycamore Street
Decatur, Georgia   30030
404-371-1236

Manufactured in the United States of America

ISBN 0-9640852-8-3

Cover and Interior Design by Paulette Livers Lambert

CONTENTS

Introduction

> How great is the love the Father has lavished on us, that we should be called children of God! And that is what we are!
>
> 1 John 3:1

Have you ever . . . . considered what it means to be a child of God? For years each Sunday, I have listened to my pastor, Rev. Frank Harrington, after baptizing a child, lift him in the air and say, "You are a child of God!" And then he always follows those words by saying, "Isn't that great?" You can almost hear the congregation as they silently answer, "Oh Yes! How wonderful! A Child of God!" And as I too am thinking how great, I am also always thinking, "Why? Why is it so great to be a child of God? What does it mean to be called a child of God?"

To answer that question, we have to look no further than to the relationships with our own children. It is an experience that no one could have ever prepared us for. We always knew there would be love and joy and lots of fun. But we were less aware of the worries, frustrations and self sacrifices. Immediately we came to learn why they say, "Raising children is not for sissies!" It is a difficult and challenging responsibility involving loving, nurturing, teaching, disciplining and providing for our children in basically whatever area that comes along in their life. It is a duty we are called to at all hours of all days whether we feel like it at the time or not! But by looking at our children, their behaviors, their growth, their "childishness," so to speak, we are able to gain much wisdom about what it means for us to be children of God.

Through the privilege of having unconditional love for our own children, we begin to comprehend the unbelievable love God has for us. Through the experiences of enduring frustrations in disciplining our own kids, the never-ending struggle to get them to do what is right, we begin to see the endless patience God has in disciplining us. Each time we provide our children food, clothing or protection, God is showing us how He provides and cares for us. Whatever, whenever, we do something as parents for our children, we must realize God is there doing the same for us. This is what it means to be a child of God.

We are His children. But our problem is that because we have grown up and are now parents ourselves, we think we no longer have a need for someone to help us to grow. We are the ones now helping others to grow. But just as your child will never outgrow you as being his or her mother, so God can never outgrow us as being our Father. He is always there nurturing, providing, guiding.

That is the point of this book, to take the universal experiences of motherhood that we know only too well, and learn from and be encouraged by them. As we translate each situation so that we become the child, we come to see ourselves as the adorable, frustrating little handfuls that the stories represent. We see what it means to be called a child of God! We are disobedient, disrespectful, in need of a ruling hand. At the same time, we are special and perfect and deserving of His love. No matter how many times we may fail, He is always there encouraging us. No matter what our needs, He watches over us. He is the One responsible for helping us to grow and to mature, as we are the ones helping our children to grow and to mature.

To raise a child is a very demanding role, one that requires much encouragement in the midst of all the daily trials that are to be faced. It is important to remember that mothers everywhere are facing the same situations we ourselves encounter. It is also important to remember that everything we are doing for our children, God is doing for us too! He has called us His children and He will be there with us along each step of our way. "How great is the love the Father has lavished on us, that we should be called children of God! And that is what we are!"

Sweet Music to My Ears

> "God saw all that he had made and it was very good."
>
> Genesis 1:31

Have you ever . . . . sat through a child's music recital? Clang! Bang! Screech! Boing! On and on it goes until you can hardly bear the noise anymore. But nonetheless, you sat through every painful moment of the recital with such love and pride that here is your wonderful child, so imperfect at what he is doing and yet so perfect in who he is.

I have laughed with friends as they have retold the stories of their children's recitals. One friend said that it sounded like her child played the same exact note for 10 minutes straight. Another said the combination of all the children playing sounded like none of them had ever even picked up the instruments prior to the recital. You can just imagine the parents all cringing and giggling to themselves at the sounds, and yet at the same time beaming with pride and with love at their precious little children doing their best.

Did you know that God feels the same way about you? The Bible tells us that after God had finished the six days of creation, He sat back on the seventh day, looked at everything He had made and saw that "it was good." At that moment He was looking directly at you. You were part of what He saw, for it says He saw "all" that he had made. When He saw you, He saw you so perfect, and He could not help but to shower His love upon you. He knew that you would have faults, that you would make lots of "noisy music" during your life. But He loved you anyhow, just as you love your child in spite of his shortcomings, weaknesses, flaws and immaturity.

It reminds me of a line from the movie "Jerry McGuire." The girl who falls in love with Jerry tells her sister that she has fallen in love with him and she tells her that she loves him "for the man that he almost is." She has a vision that others cannot see of him becoming a perfect man. I feel that is how God sees us, for the person who we almost are and for that He loves us, beyond what words can describe and in spite of our faults!

It is so comforting that God can see us so perfectly. And when I doubt that He can love me because of the wretched "music" I make, those times when I know I have done the wrong thing, "played the wrong note," I am reminded of a secret He whispered in my ear some years ago. I was beating myself up for something I had done wrong and the Holy Spirit quietly said, "Margaret, I wish you could see yourself the way that I see you." I believe God sees me as good and beautiful and perfect, and He sees you that way too. Not because of anything we have done but because He is our Father, He loves us and He has the vision to see us as the person who we will one day become.

Let Me Count the Ways

> We love because he first loved us.
>
> 1 John 4:19

Have you ever . . . . thought about all of the things you do for your child that should cause him to love you? A friend of mine plays a game with her children called "Let Me Count The Ways" where they tell each other all the reasons they love each other. One day I decided to play this with my two boys and I asked them to tell me the reasons why they loved me. And their simple, most basic response was, "Because you love us."

Well, I thought that was sort of boring. I was looking for answers like "because you buy our clothes and food, because you take us to the store for treats, because you are always there when we need you, because you let our friends come over to play." So pridefully I said again, "No really, tell me the reasons why you love me." And again they stated, very mat-ter-of-factly, "We love you, because you love us."

My kids were really saying, "Mommy, we love you because you showed us the experience of what it is to love and be loved and now we want that as a part of our lives too." Simple as pie! It was not the things I was "doing" for them but the way I was "being" with them. Through a sacrificial, often unappreciated, no holds-barred kind of love they were able to see what love looks and feels and tastes like, and they wanted to model that for their own lives.

Now I realize that is how it is with God. We come to love Him and love others because He loves us first. He shows us what it looks like to love. That is the whole message of the Bible. But He doesn't want us to love Him merely for what He gives us and does for us. He wants us to love Him and others as a response to coming to know what love is and for being thankful for that experience.

Love is not created by a tally sheet that says the depth of our love is based on the criteria of the needs He meets for us. Love is a simple response that says, "Yes, this is good. I will pass this on to you and to others regardless of what else you will do for me." Remember the next time you begin to question God's love for you, when you get bogged down in "what has He done for you lately" type-thinking, that you have a choice to make. Will you love Him regardless of your circumstances merely for the fact that He confesses His love for you?

The Joy of Your Company

> *By day the Lord directs his love, at night his song is with me—a prayer to the God of my life.*
>
> *Psalm 42:8*

Have you ever . . . . had a few moments just to play with your child? You weren't teaching or disciplining him or solving any of life's problems, you were just playing and enjoying each other's company. When Brandon, my second child, was a baby I can remember having the best time with him when I went to put him to bed. We would go into his room and I would sit in the rocking chair in an attempt to rock him to sleep. And inevitably he would start "messing" with me. Acting like he was falling asleep on my shoulder, he would slyly reach up and poke my eyeballs with his fingers or say silly, made-up words and I of course would giggle, thus making it all the more fun for him to do it over and over. He always knew it would get a chuckle from me and that it would prolong his bed time. And the five extra minutes were always well worth it to me. Just having quiet time between the two of us—laughing, joking, but most importantly, bonding a relationship between us—was a valuable part of our day!

This is what God desires from us when He asks us to come to Him in prayer and have quiet time with Him. It is not always just to teach us things to "change" our lives, but rather to build that important bond. God is steadfast in His love for us and He is always there, but often we allow ourselves to believe He is far off, only there for the big issues of life. But just as every moment with our children is not spent in teaching principles and disciplining them, so not every moment with God is spent in teaching or rebuking.

As my relationship with my children has been developed through the years, I have come to see how important time is in building trust and love and devotion to one another. My children and I respond to one another because there are good times and bad times, but mostly together times. And that is how our relationship of trust and love and devotion is to be with God. It is developed as we spend time with Him, getting to know Him and sharing the intimacies of our lives. As I share the experiences of each day with my children, so I share each day with God, revealing my most personal experiences, joys and disappointments. The more time you spend just being with Him, the greater your relationship will be, and the more joy you will have in your life as a result of being in His company.

Could You Give Him Up?

> For God so loved the world that he gave his one and only Son, that whoever believes in him shall not perish but have eternal life.
>
> John 3:16

Have you ever . . . said you loved your child so much that you would die for him? I remember one time my son was facing the possibility of surgery and my husband and I both saying we wished it was us rather than him. We would rather face the possibility of pain ourselves, even the possibility of death, than to have our child face it. Well that was very noble for us as parents to say we could give up our own lives. But the real question of love would be if we could give up our own child to save the life of another. Could we be so noble as to do that?

Could we look in the face of a child, whom we could never love as our own, and determine to sacrifice our beloved to save the life of another? I doubt it very seriously! I doubt any one of us could be that sacrificial. "But," you say, "that is different. I love my own child enough to die for him. I am not talking about anyone else's child." Think about how hard it would be, especially if that person was not even a good person! Think about what kind of passionate, Christ-like love you would have to have for someone to do that. Imagine losing your only child.

But that's exactly what God did. He took his only Son, Jesus, born to the world and allowed Him to die so that all the rest of us could live—so that we could have an abundant life on earth as well as an eternal life with Him in heaven. I often take for granted the sacrifice God made. The pain of separation He must have felt at Jesus's crucifixion can't even be imagined. But that is true love, Godly love. It leaves no room for doubt.

God loves you and me and everyone who believes that Jesus is His son. It is a love that is completely incomprehensible, especially in light of our own behaviors. God didn't decide to help someone just because he was good. No, Christ came to save both the lovely and the unlovely. What is your response to that kind of love? A love that doesn't care whether you are good or bad, but just wants you to be redeemed. I pray that you will claim that love. Thank Him and live your life abundantly knowing nothing can take that away.

Just Remember I Will Always Love You

For I am convinced that neither death nor life, neither angels nor demons, neither the present nor the future, nor any powers, neither height nor depth, nor anything else in all creation, will be able to separate us from the love of God that is in Christ Jesus our Lord.
Romans 8:38,39

Have you ever . . . had to face a time of separation from your child? The types of separation could range from the time when she is at school, to more extended times like vacation, or even situations like divorce where you did not have full custody of her? But whether that time apart was a natural part of her growing life or whether it is was due to a tragic situation, it resulted in a time of anxiety because you yearned to be with them and yet, for the time being, couldn't. My constant fear when the kids are not in my presence is, "What is happening to them? Are they O.K.?" And my prayer, when they are away, is that wherever they may be or whatever comes their way, they will always know that I love them.

I'm sure every mother, if given the chance to give final words to her child, would utter these words: "Just remember, I will always love you." There is promise and strength, hope and comfort in these words. They say that no matter what, there is nothing that can stand in the way of my love for you.

I've never faced anything frightening with my children. My husband and I are married. We are alive! And, blessedly, our children have not experienced tragedy in their lives. But there is always that "what if" that lingers from hearing too many real life horror stories. What if someone abducted them and they couldn't be found? What if they were sexually molested? What if my husband or I were to die? What would carry our children through these times? I pray it would be their knowledge of my absolute love for them. I pray they would know that through thick or thin I would do all in my power to help them.

But did you know God loves us that much too? Even more! And the apostle Paul shares with us the depth of God's love here as he states NOTHING can separate us from God's love. Nothing in your past, nothing in your present can separate you from His loving you. No fears, no worries, no doubts, no sins. Not heaven or hell, not good actions or bad, not doing too little nor doing too much will keep you from His love. He is always there ready for you to be assured of His undying love for you. No matter what comes your way He is there. Just remember He will always love you!

Tough Love

Hear, O earth: I am bringing disaster on this people, the fruit of their schemes, because they have not listened to my words and have rejected my law.

Jeremiah 6:19

Have you ever... had a child or a friend or any one close to you who has struggled with a destructive addiction? One of my best friends in college was addicted to alcohol and drugs. When she was straight, she was one of the all-time best people you could imagine. This was precisely the reason I tolerated the other side of her dual personality, which was when she was "wasted" and totally out of control: irresponsible, loud, embarrassing, seeking only her own agenda. Each time she would binge she would feel horrible when she started to sober up. The guilt would be enormous, and yet as much as all those who loved her tried to help, she would continue in her self-destruction. We all tried to help, especially her parents, because we so dearly loved her and didn't want to see her destroyed. Yet, in spite of our efforts, she was eventually destroyed. She lost her husband, her only child, and many friends along the way. Eventually, everyone had had enough and left her to her self-destruction.

The rehabilitation centers label this "tough love." It is simply that we as friends and loved ones can not continue to support her by picking up after her mess. She would have to learn to do that herself.

In the days before Jerusalem's exiles, God was the one who continued to pick up Israel's broken pieces. He warned them through prophets that they had to turn from their self-destructive lifestyles. But they continued on in their self-fulfilling ways just as an addict will do. They would sin and God would be there to help them return from their troubles. But after enough times He said, "Enough! I can no longer show compassion." And His tough love began on His chosen people in a way only God can do.

He had to let them learn on their own that they could not continue to lead an unrighteous life and expect not to be punished. And we today must know that God will certainly bring His tough love upon us, just as He did to Jerusalem, when we continue in self-serving, destructive lifestyles. God is merciful and just, but when necessary, He does respond with tough love. Thankfully, when we do repent and renew our ways, He is quick and faithful to forgive. But we must renew our ways just as the addict must renew his actions to be taken back into His loving arms.

Hide and Go Seek

You will seek me and find me when you seek me with all your heart.

Jeremiah 29:13

Have you ever . . . played hide and go seek with your children? In my home, my kids loved to do the hiding and always wanted me to come and search for them. They would run and hide and then there would always be a great thrill as they were discovered. As you can imagine, it wasn't hard to find them as they slammed closet doors or moved the sofa to squeeze underneath. But even if I knew exactly where they were, I would make it a suspenseful game by looking in other places just to make them excited thinking I couldn't find them.

Our pursuit of God is like hide and go seek, only He is the one hiding in a not-so-hard to find place. Unlike our children, He is not trying to be sneaky. He gives us clues as to where He is, like the clues of children giggling behind the curtains. As we learn the sound of His voice, the size of His nature, the sight of places where He can go, the easier He is to find.

But we are like mothers looking in the wrong places. He is right there waiting to be found, and yet we continue to look everywhere except where we know we should. We look for Him in our decorated homes and fancy cars. We look for Him in our extracurricular activities. We look for Him in careers. We look for Him in fame and recognition. But the only place we will ever find Him is within our hearts.

God wants us to find Him. The game for Him is in the discovery. He waits anxiously for the time when He can say, "Surprise—you found me!" We've got to quit picking up sofa cushions and looking behind curtains. Quit the halfway attempts and begin the single-minded, determined search He wants from us. The search begins as He is revealed in His Word. To find Him you must first know what you are looking for. He won't be found in the things of the world. His ways are much different. But as you seek, you will find, because the irony of it all is that the whole time you are looking He is right before your eyes!

You Da Mom!

*Great is the Lord and
most worthy of praise.
Psalm 145:3*

Have you ever . . . done something special for a group of kids and just been elated by the thanks they gave you? I often like to pick my kids up at school and ask them if they would like to go for some ice cream. Of course the screams from the back seat overpower me as we zip off for our treat. And not always, but often enough, on the way home the kids sing my praises and shout, "You da Mom!"

I don't take them for special treats just to get praises, but when they do, it is especially rewarding for me. It makes me feel great that they are appreciative and thankful for what they have received. It is a way that I see that they are aware of their blessings, their good fortune.

It is the same way with God. We should be praising and thanking Him all day every day for the many good gifts He has given us. If nothing else, we should be giving our praise daily just for the gift of His ever-present love and mercy upon us. I know that God does not give us these gifts just to have us bow down before Him in praise, but that should be our natural response. We should sing praises for His marvelous creation. We should praise Him for His peace and compassion, His greatness and life beyond discovery. We should shout His great name with joy and excitement that we can even be in His presence.

The words thank you are such simple words and yet they reveal so much. They show our appreciation, our acknowledgment that we have been the beneficiaries of something good. We don't have to wait for something extraordinarily good to happen to us to give thanks. Wonderful things happen all day when God is the focus of your life. So be sure and thank Him, acknowledge how awesome He truly is. Don't stop with the usual thanksgiving of a meal or for the chance at a new day, but take time to see where God is truly "Da Man" in your life.

The opportunities to praise and thank God are infinite. Just think about all the times when you would love for your children to give you thanks: fixing meals, picking up toys, cleaning and ironing clothes, keeping the pantry stocked with snacks for their friends. God's work in our lives is infinitely greater than these things we do. Be astounded and wowed and appreciative— and then tell Him. Praise Him all day long!

Discerning Voices

My sheep listen to my voice; I know them, and they follow me.
John 10:27

Have you ever . . . been in a crowded place and lost track of your child? Even if for just an instant, you panic. You begin frantically to look for him and you begin to call his name out loud. Over and over you call his name, at first in a normal tone of voice but eventually in a panic, you begin to scream. And suddenly, in the midst of all the noise—the people talking, music playing, intercoms squawking and machines humming—you hear the sound of your child saying, "Here I am, over here." Oh my gosh! What a relief! You can just feel the release of the fear that had just overcome you in that brief but terrifying moment of separation.

But in the midst of all that noise, did you ever stop and consider how your child knew to answer you? There are lots of people around, different parents each calling for their own children, noises competing for their attention. How did your child know to answer? It is because he knows the sound of your voice. And he knows that if you are calling, he had best be wise and respond. The relationship and bond that has been built over a life-time has allowed him to know, without a doubt, the voice of his own mother calling.

What does this say to us about being God's children? It says we must know His voice and we must be aware of when He is calling us. We must be able to hear Him when He calls to give us directions, when He tells us it is time for a certain activity or simply when He calls to tell us we've wandered off. It says that we must stay close to Him and listen for Him so as not to get lost.

We must be able to discern God's voice so we know it is Him when He calls. Satan will try and disguise his voice and lead us away from our Heavenly Father. If we have not spent the time in coming to know God's voice, we can easily be deceived. We may find ourselves running to the wrong voice, leaving us in a dangerous situation. Just as you want to be 100 percent sure your child will answer only to you, God wants to be sure you answer only to Him. As you spend time in coming to know Him, you will become more and more discerning to hear when He is calling.

Skinned Knees

He will wipe every tear from their eyes. There will be no more death or mourning or crying or pain, for the old order of things has passed away.
Revelation 21:4

Have you ever . . . had your child come running to you after she has taken a spill on the cement? Bicycle crashes, running around the swimming pool, playing chase in the driveway all bring up visions of scraped-up knees, noses, elbows and chins. But what is the first thing when your child comes running in the house that she wants from you? Even more than a Band-Aid or some medicine to take away the pain, she wants her mother's loving arms. She wants to run to the one who will pick her up and promise that everything is going to be all right.

It's what we all want—little and big children— when we are hurt, or scared or sick or beaten up. We want our mommies! We want our moms to be the ones who will wipe away our tears. We want them just to be there for us. We want the reassurance that the present sting of our pain will indeed go away. We want to hear the words of comfort and compassion, to feel the warmth of hugs.

God is just like our mommy, only infinitely better. He promises to wipe away all our tears and that we can look forward to a time when we won't ever experience pain again. As a parent we promise that everything will be O.K.—that the pain will subside. And we want to believe in our own promises. But God is the only One whose promises we can be assured of. He promises that there will come a day when we will no longer experience any pain or suffering or grief or illness.

All of us will suffer a lot of bumps and bruises and skinned knees as we go through life, most of them not being of the physical nature. We may face the pain of death, broken relationships, financial difficulties, or children gone astray. But just as we pick up our children and wipe away their tears, so does God, the ultimate loving parent, promise to wipe away every tear from our eyes. Every sorrow and every pain we experience He will comfort. Every "skinned knee" He will heal because God is the Father of compassion over pain. He is the God who promises to bring us back to full restoration with Him. He promises us it will all be O.K.

You Just Don't Understand!

> For we do not have a high priest who is unable to sympathize with our weaknesses, but we have one who has been tempted in every way, just as we are— yet was without sin.
>
> Hebrews 4:15

Have you ever . . . had your child say to you, "Mo-o-o-om [drawn out for emphasis!], you just don't understand!"? Understand what? Here they are, babes in the woods, and they're thinking "There is no possible way this old fogy could ever understand what is going on in my life!" How could they think that? Is it impossible to believe that mothers were once children too? Would they die of surprise to know that we do understand, that we have been there?

Every now and then, my mother reminisces over the years that my brothers and I became teenagers. She laughs about how she was made to feel like she had all of a sudden became so clueless. She didn't feel like anything strange had happened to her, that she'd all of a sudden gone stupid, but we kept telling her, "You just don't understand!" So maybe, she figured, there was something she was missing, that she didn't understand.

I can remember during those years, just as my kids say to me now, I would say, "Mom. You just don't understand. All the other girls are staying out late.

And they all get to wear their mother's clothes." And I know my mom just chuckled thinking, "Right, I don't understand! I've never been a teenage girl myself!" In hindsight, I realize, she did understand and that's why her answers were always the way they were. Because she understood, because she had been where I was, she could sympathize and at the same time she could be the strength in the midst of my weakness.

That is exactly the same situation we have with Jesus. He's been through every situation that we have. We can't look to Him and say, "You just don't understand." Because He does. Even though He is God, He was still a man. He faced the same weaknesses and temptations that we do. It has given Him the ability to be sympathetic, merciful and helpful.

I used to feel that He just couldn't understand how difficult it was to be a mother, but He can. God revealed to me through Scripture that Jesus had many more "children" clinging to Him for nurturing, advice and help than I ever could imagine. And yet look at the way He handled it. In any situation you may find yourself without the skills to cope, go to Jesus and ask for His help. I promise, He will understand.

Tweezing Splinters

> *I am the true vine, and my Father is the gardener. He cuts off every branch in me that bears no fruit, while every branch that does bear fruit he prunes so that it will be even more fruitful.*
> John 15:1,2

Have you ever . . . tried to tweeze a splinter out of a child's foot? I can think of several times when my children got splinters and the awful scenes that followed. My husband and I would try to hold them down in an effort to pull the splinters out, and the kids would scream and cry. They knew that pain was on its way. We were upset because we knew we were going to have to cause them pain. Everyone was miserable! And yet everyone knew that the splinter had to come out.

My kids always beg us to just leave the splinter alone. "It will fall out on its own," they cry. They just can't bear to go through the process of removal. But the reality is that even if we did ignore it for awhile, eventually it has to come out. If not, the seemingly small splinter can turn into an infection that eventually affects everything around it.

It is the same thing when God tries to remove seemingly small "splinters" from our lives. We know and God knows that certain areas of our lives are causing our whole body infection, and yet we just can't stand the pain and fear of removing them. I can think of bad habits I've had, bad friendships and wrong thinking that I knew God wanted me to get rid of. And yet when He came with His tweezers, or as it says here, His pruning shears, I completely ran in the opposite direction. I screamed and cried and kicked because I didn't want to have to let go of my little "splinters." I didn't want to have to face what I thought would be too much pain in the way of self-sacrifice to give them up. I thought I would simply rather live with the current pain than face the unknown pain of removal.

But complete removal of sin in our lives is the only answer. God won't allow us to walk around with infection in our bodies. There is no way we will ever flower and produce good fruit when we have these foreign particles living within us. He does not try to remove these sore spots in our lives to punish us, but rather to heal us, to make us stronger. If He did not prune and tweeze our lives constantly, we would have no chance at healthy, vibrant, fruitful lives.

Change is hard. We don't like to give up what we are familiar with, but God is the perfect physician. He knows what is healthy for us. He knows if something is harmful to us and needs to be removed. Trust in God. Let Him take those harmful areas away. The sooner you submit, relax and face the pain, the easier the tweezing process will be and the faster the healing will begin!

Oblivious to the Call

> Hear this, you foolish
> and senseless people,
> who have eyes but do not
> see, who have ears but
> do not hear.
>
> Jeremiah 5:21

Have you ever . . . called your child's name while he was watching television and gotten absolutely no response? Over and over you called with not even a turn of the head or an eyebrow raised in response. When this happens, I want to go over and shake him and say "Excuse me, don't you hear me calling?" And what usually ends up happening is I begin screaming the child's name at the top of my lungs, with total disbelief that he would have so little regard as to not even respond. It is unthinkable to me that someone I have loved and raised would not even have the courtesy to answer with a simple "Yes, Mom?"

In the Old Testament, we hear God calling the people of Israel like this over and over through various prophets. He calls, "Israel, Israel," and nothing. No response. He so desires for them to answer, to quit tuning Him out, but they go right on about their business, too consumed in their own selfish desires to listen. I'm sure for God it was also unthinkable that His people would not answer His call. The ones He had loved and raised and protected could so easily ignore Him. But their day of punishment would soon come, as their lack of listening eventually resulted in virtual destruction and takeovers by various armies. They received harsh punishment because they chose not to hear the things God was saying.

The same situation still happens to us today as we ourselves ignore God's callings. Although usually not in the form of a takeover of nations, destruction of some sort overcomes us when we shut God out. He calls and calls, but often we are too preoccupied to answer. And so He is left with no recourse but to punish us. Whether it is having trouble on your job, being in trouble financially or fighting with someone you love, God uses punishment to finally get your attention. He punishes us to get us to understand the need to respect Him enough to answer when He calls.

But in our own foolishness, we ignore Him. We shut Him out as a child does to us when he is engaged in watching T.V. We allow ourselves to have selective hearing. If we think we are about to hear good news, we respond. If it is a word that is contrary to what we want to do, we ignore Him. But you can't put God off forever. When you become His child, you are responsible to answer Him or, as the Israelites saw, to face the punishment. God won't allow disrespectful children in His home. When you hear His voice deep within your soul calling you, for whatever reason it may be, just answer. All you need do is just ask, "Yes, Lord?" You will receive His patience and mercy and favor if you do not put Him off!

Mother's Day Presents

> You do not delight in sacrifice, or I would bring it; you do not take pleasure in burnt offerings. The sacrifices of God are a broken spirit; a broken and contrite heart.
>
> Psalm 51:16-17

Have you ever... had your child buy you a totally pointless gift for Mother's Day? I can remember how awful the day before Mother's Day was when I was growing up. I would find myself panicking in the local hardware gift shop, trying to find a gift for my mom that was not too expensive, yet would not make me look too cheap. And I always remember feeling a little guilty giving it to her because I knew I had only made a half-hearted effort to find her something. When she received it she would always smile and say thank you and then quietly put the gift away, never to be seen again. But prior to ever buying the gift I could recall my mother saying, "You don't have to buy me anything. All I really want is your love." But I just couldn't understand what she meant.

I used to think she was so corny in not wanting a gift. "Who wouldn't want a gift if they were due one?" I thought. And only now, as a parent myself, do I understand what she meant. It wasn't something material she wanted. There was nothing I could buy her that she couldn't buy for herself. What she wanted was a gift that came personally and lovingly from me. Something that only I could give—something from my heart.

It is the same way with God. He doesn't want something materialistic. He wants something from our hearts. He doesn't want a gift just because we are supposed to give one. He doesn't want us to give our money away because we have guilt upon our shoulders. What He wants is "a broken spirit; a broken and contrite heart." The kind of gifts that are pleasing to God are: when we refuse to talk bad about someone, when we are content with what we have rather than being jealous, when we help someone even if it inconveniences us a bit, when we do what He asks us to do.

The outward, tangible gifts mean nothing, but the inward acts from an obedient heart give Him great joy. I know my children love me when I see them obeying me, when they give me something because they want to and not because someone tells them they have to. For me, a real Mother's Day gift does not come on Mother's Day, but on every day that their hearts are devoted to doing the right thing. In the same way, a real gift to God does not come from a one-time donation of our time or money, but in our day-to-day commitment in humbling ourselves and following Him. When we give our hearts to God to let Him mold them as He pleases, this is the most delightful, pleasurable gift we can give!

The Law of the Land

The law of the Lord is perfect, reviving the soul.

Psalm 19:7

Have you ever . . . heard that kids love discipline? My husband always used to say that to me and I would just laugh. He came from a stricter upbringing than I did and I simply could not believe that children would WANT discipline! I thought that the freer you were to make your own choices, the better off you were. The problem with my plan was that too much freedom got me into trouble. I had no parameters on which to base my decisions.

But as a parent myself, I now see his point. Children do desire and need to know the "law of the land." When I have no ground rules for my kids, all chaos breaks loose. My kids become unruly, self-centered and disrespectful. In order to avoid this, I must set rules to follow. Rules like: no foul language, no leaving the house without telling an adult, no eating snacks before dinner. They are rules that at times may seem silly, rules that my children naturally don't want to abide by, yet rules that provide a way to help them to live at peace within society, as well as keep them safe.

When God gave us His law, it was for our own good too, so that we would not hurt ourselves and so we could live at peace amongst each other. He did not set the law to keep us from having a good time, but rather to give us instruction on how we should live our lives. When we attempt to walk without any of His direction, we end up stumbling and finding ourselves in trouble. But when we follow His law, we find protection from harm. We find joy and fulfillment.

I once heard the comedian Jerry Seinfeld say he was glad to be an adult because he could finally determine how many cookies he could eat at one sitting without someone saying, "Just one more." I got tickled at that because it's true our rules do sometimes seem silly, but we have them to teach, to give instruction and to bring about wisdom. I'm sure Seinfeld's mother didn't really care how many cookies he ate, but she did care that he learned self-control. She cared that he learn the rules that bring the body good and not harm.

As we mature in our walk with God, we must learn what God's law is and come to understand how it actually does set us free rather than bind us in. As we read the Bible we learn what the rules are. As we obey them we gain lives that are blameless and pure. That is when the real freedom comes about. True freedom does not come about by having no rules, but by following the rules of the One who is wiser, more knowledgeable than all, the rules of the One who has seen it all and knows the best path!

Don't! Stop! Quit!

God disciplines us for our good, that we may share in his holiness. No discipline seems pleasant at the time, but painful. Later on, however, it produces a harvest of righteousness and peace for those who have been trained by it.
Hebrews 12:10, 11

Have you ever . . . become frustrated and worn down in disciplining your child, feeling that all of your efforts in rebuking him will never pay off? Sometimes I feel that all I do is correct my kids. "Don't do that!" "Stop it!" "No!" "Quit it!" I am giving orders like a broken record in an effort to teach them right from wrong and their response is either to ignore me or to hate me because I am so "demanding." It's frustrating, painful and unrewarding.

But slowly, as the years pass by, the task of disciplining does become rewarding. I can remember, to my amazement and delight, when my children automatically were saying, "Yes, sir" and "Please" and "Thank you," all without my prompting them. A few more years went by and they began to take off their hats at the dinner table. They stuck their hands out voluntarily to shake someone else's hand and they would let others have their way before them. Teeth were being brushed and beds made without my constant threats of cavities and no allowance. And slowly, inch by inch, I began to realize that discipline does pay off! All of the "don'ts" and "stops" and "quit its" were producing what I had dreamed they would produce. My kids had changed from terrors I feared to take in public to young gentlemen I was proud to show off to my friends.

The disciplining process can be just as frustrating for us as children of God. He tells us, "Don't!" "Stop!" "Quit it!" We kick and scream and fight, because our natural tendency is to be undisciplined. But slowly, again inch by inch, we begin to see the process of disciplining paying off in our own lives. To our own amazement, what God has said to stop, we have stopped; what He has said to do, we have done.

My mother always used to say she loved us too much to allow us to act unruly. What she did to keep us walking down the straight and narrow path was for our own good, whether we liked it or not. She was shaping people of character. And so is God in His infinite love creating people of character out of us as He enforces His discipline upon us. He loves us too much to let us be uncontrolled, self-satisfying children. I encourage you to realize that God disciplines you and me because He loves us. He wants to make us people of great character. The process can be lengthy. God doesn't tell us something one time and we automatically are obedient. Sometimes He has to say it over and over and over. But just as with our kids, the rewards become abundant as little by little we become more mature, controlled and wise.

Because 1 Said So!

Moses said to God, "Suppose I get to the Israelites and say to them 'The God of your fathers has sent me to you,' and they ask me, 'What is his name?' Then what shall I tell them?" God said to Moses, "I Am Who I Am."
Exodus 3:13, 14

Have you ever . . . had your child ask you why he had to do something? "Why do I have to pick up my clothes?" "Why do I have to go to church?" "Why do I have to write thank-you notes?" Why is almost a knee-jerk response to any command I give as a parent. Of course I want to say, "Why can't you just do what you are told without asking so many questions?" But instead, to let them know I mean business, I respond, "Because I said so!"

Now for the most part, I want to be fair with my children. If they want to learn about how something works or if they genuinely need more information on a particular subject, I am happy to answer questions. But often the "Whys" my kids are asking are not to learn more information, but are done to question my authority. The "Why" becomes a form of nagging indicating that the task at hand is no fun and they are going to drag their heels. And when it is said in this way, the only answer that suffices is "Because I said so!" It is the final authority. It is the statement that says, "I know you don't like this but this is how it is." No arguments, no stalling—just do it!

You know God has that final authority over us too. We go to Him asking "Why?" in an effort to avoid doing the things He asks. "Why do I have to deny myself?" "Why do I have to treat others as myself?" "Why can't I just do as I please?" We already know the answer in our hearts, but we are just biding time, stalling the inevitable.

In Exodus, when Moses feared telling the Israelites Who had sent him, God told him to say, "I Am" had sent him. God called Himself, "I Am Who I Am." His name was to be the final authority. It was to command fear, reverence and obedience. It was His name then and remains true today. Because we can come to Him personally, we sometimes forget that He is Jehovah, God Almighty. And so we boldly confront Him with our own "Whys?" But if God tells us to do something, we are wasting our breath when we ask "Why?" He will only remind us that He is, "I Am." He will rebuke us for asking the question and say, "Because I say so." Don't ever forget His authority and His power. The sooner you subside to His will, the sooner you will reap His rewards.

You Are Grounded!

The Lord replied, "I have forgiven them, as you asked. Nevertheless, as surely as I live and as surely as the glory of the Lord fills the whole earth, not one of the men who saw my glory and the miraculous signs I performed in Egypt and in the desert but who disobeyed me and tested me ten times—not one of them will ever see the land I promised on oath to their forefathers."

Numbers 14:20-23

The Lord has taken away your sin. You are not going to die. But because by doing this . . . the son born to you will die.

2 Samuel 12:13, 14

Have you ever . . . had to ground your child? My husband and I had this "privilege" recently with our five-year-old son. He had gone on a spree of using the scissors on things other than paper: his younger brother's shirt, his younger brother's finger and finally on a bean bag chair filled with mounds of tiny "balls of snow" he gleefully threw around the room. Now my husband and I knew we had to punish him—but what exactly is appropriate "grounding" for a five year old?

After much thought, and laughter at the thought of having to "ground" a five year old, we decided upon a relative punishment of no friends to play with for five days! We decided that even at five years of age, our son was ready to learn about making wise decisions and that actions have consequences, especially after having had repeated warnings.

Naturally my husband and I were furious when we found out about his misuse of the scissors on the bean bag and my son knew he was in big trouble! He begged in his panicked little voice, "Forgive me, Mommy. I promise I won't do it again." But we knew these incidents were no mere accidents. He had willingly chosen to do as he pleased over what he knew was right. Although we assured him he was indeed forgiven, at the same time, we were firm in teaching that even if you make mistakes and you are sorry, there is still a price to pay.

The Israelites in the Old Testament were poster children examples of what it meant to be "grounded." Over and over they made mistakes for which they begged for God's mercy. And they would always receive it along with a good dose of punishment. Captivity and slavery, not getting to see the promised land, the personal loss to King David of a son are but a few examples of their punishments. They repented and were given a reprieve to come back into fellowship with God, but that reprieve could not undo their punishment.

We hear of God's great mercy, his power to forgive and to cleanse completely. But this is not our license into selfish living. Actions have consequences. God wants your actions to be good so that He may bless you. But if you continually defy Him to his face, he will ground you. He will give you a wake-up call to remind you of the life He wants you to lead. Don't be fooled that His grace is your passport to sin. His holiness cannot be compromised and in your effort to choose your will over His, you will face the consequences.

I'm Too Scared

Through the fear of the Lord a man avoids evil.

Proverbs 16:6

Have you ever . . . had your kids not do something bad for fear of what you would do to them as punishment? They knew that if they engaged in a certain "naughty" activity, they were going to be in big trouble. For example, I never had a problem with my children coloring on our walls. It was just one of those things they knew would absolutely make me crazy. So, because of their fear of me, they just never did it. Another example would be how I avoided, as a teenager, ever using my parents' credit cards without first asking. I would have been petrified of what they would have done to me, and so I never used them without their permission. Through the fear of our parents, we avoid evil!

But the Bible says, "Through the fear of the Lord a man avoids evil." Are there certain activities we avoid for fear of what God will do to us? Just as our children, there are times when we are fearful and times when we're not. We tend to fear God in avoiding the BIG sins but are a little more lenient when it comes to the small ones. For example, God says, "Don't murder. Don't steal. Don't have sexual relationships with someone else's spouse." But He also says, "Don't gossip. Don't tell lies. Don't be greedy." In our hearts, we absolutely know not to commit murder. We know that the wrath of God will surely come upon us with this sin. But why are we more risky when it comes to gossip, lies and greed? Because just as our children, when we don't immediately see the consequences of our sins, we are fooled into thinking they will not do us as much harm. But I promise you God does get mad about these and we will see a time when He will punish us for even the small sins.

"Through the fear of the Lord a man avoids evil." We are to fear God both for what He can do to us as well as because His name commands profound respect. We should avoid doing the things He says not to do for no other reason than because of our reverence for Him. Jeremiah 32:40 says, "I will inspire them to fear me." Just as parents want their children to fear and obey them in everything out of a proper respect, so God desires our fear and respect. So here is the challenge for you: Seek to evaluate your true fear of God. Are you mingling in dangerous waters unaware of your potential harm? Are you sinning and slapping Him in the face? Or are you fearful enough to avoid what He clearly tells you to not to do?

House Rules and Automatic Spankings

Choose for yourselves this day whom you will serve. . . But as for me and my household, we will serve the Lord.

Joshua 24:15

Have you ever . . . had certain rules in your home that you expected your children to live by? "House Rules," so to speak, which are the guidelines and boundaries that everyone in your home is expected to follow. One of our many "house rules" is that there is to be no spitting. My children have learned the hard way that they must abide by that rule, or they get an "automatic spanking"! It all started one day when they came home from school spitting on each other. Well, it just infuriated me! So I told them, "In this household, there will be no spitting—not as a joke, not when playing with our friends, NEVER! And if you do spit, you will get an automatic spanking. No warnings. No questions asked. Automatic spanking!" Now the rules had been set and the time had come. They could choose to obey me or they could choose to spit, but they knew without a doubt what the consequences would be for either choice.

God gives us the choice to obey His "house rules" as well. From the moment we hear Christ saying, "Follow me," we have a decision to make. We can either do what He says or we can serve ourselves, but

either way we choose we will experience consequences. Deuteronomy 11:26 says,

> *"See, I am setting before you today a blessing
> and a curse—the blessing if you obey the com-
> mands of the Lord your God . . . ; the curse if you
> disobey the commands of the Lord your God."*

In any choice we are given, God presents a "blessing
and a curse," according to our obedience or disobedience. It is His way of warning us and helping us to
avoid an automatic spanking. The Bible is full of
these "blessings and curses" handed down to His
children. Abraham received a blessing as he chose to
follow God. David received a curse when He took
Bathsheba in his bed. Adam and Eve—well, we all
know about the curse placed on them as a result of
their disobedience!

Daily we have a choice whether to serve and
follow God or to do as we please. And just as our children must do, we must weigh the consequences of our
actions. Will we choose Satan with his "do what you
want, when you want" attitude, knowing it will make
our heavenly Father upset? Or will we be fearful
enough to follow God's rules and avoid the possibility
of a "spanking"?

You Can't Come to My Birthday Party!

We should not commit sexual immorality, as some of them did—and in one day twenty-three thousand of them died. We should not test the Lord, as some of them did—and were killed by snakes. And do not grumble, as some of them did—and were killed by the destroying angel. These things happened to them as examples and were written down as warnings for us, on whom the fulfillment of the ages has come.
1 Corinthians 10:8-11

Have you ever . . . had to threaten your child to get him to do something? I realized the other day how out of hand my threats had become when my three-year-old son threatened that I could not come to his birthday party if I did not come help him pick up his clothes. Although I was shocked that he had the nerve to threaten me, it didn't take a rocket scientist to figure out where he had learned the art of making such threats. It seems I am always threatening them, "If you don't, ... I'm going to ...." And though I hate to resort to this tactic, often I feel I am left with no other choice. The only thing that gets them to act right is to threaten them with punishment.

We can sit around all day hoping our kids will be driven by the carrot rather than the stick, that they will do what we ask for the reward rather than the rod, but in the end it usually fails. Kids don't take the time to evaluate the warnings you give them. You can tell them one hundred times, "Look what happened to your brother when he did this. Don't do it or the same thing will happen to you." But it is not until the punishment is actually placed upon them that they wish they had chosen to do right and avoid the wrong.

In this Scripture, Paul gives the Corinthians their own threat. He recounts a series of disasters that happened to the Israelites while they wandered in the desert and says, "Watch out or this could happen to you too." The Israelites were worshipping other gods, having sexually immoral relationships, testing God and grumbling. As a result, in one day 23,000 died, some were killed by snakes and others killed by the destroying angel. These were no idle threats. God was serious about His children doing what He told them to do. In essence He says, "Don't make me threaten you! Just do what I say."

But we are all so hard-headed—the Corinthians, our children and ultimately each one of us. Instead of doing what we are supposed to do, we smugly go about our own selfish ways not really believing God will harm us. But the threat before us is that what happened to them could also happen to us. Don't test God. Don't try His patience because although He is a loving God, He is also a God who demands obedience. Look at the way He punished our forefathers and take heed.

Running Away from Home

From this time many of his disciples turned back and no longer followed him. "You do not want to leave too, do you?" Jesus asked the Twelve. Simon Peter answered him, "Lord, to whom shall we go?"
John 6:66-68

Have you ever . . . had your child threaten to run away from home? In a huff, furious at you for who-knows-what, she marches to her room, packs a bag full of clothes and sneaks out the door! You know what is going on the whole time but play dumb. She meanwhile is imagining your horror in discovering her disappearance, and the guilt you will feel at having done to her whatever it was you did!

But as night rolls in and she begins to get lonely and hungry curled up under the next-door neighbor's bush, her imagination begins to wander. "Who will help me if a stranger comes along in the dark? Where am I going to get something to eat? Will I ever see my brothers and sisters again?" And suddenly home doesn't look so bad after all. Whatever it was that seemed so bad to make her run away doesn't look so bad in relation to being out in the dark all alone! And, so frustrated that she couldn't live alone, frightened of being in the dark, rustling bushes, she slowly makes her way back home.

And so it goes with this question, "To whom shall we go?" Is the life we live with Christ better than the one we would live without Him? Even if we may be mad at God, even if we may not like the things He is asking (or forcing) us to do, even if we may think the teachings of Jesus are too hard, would we rather dwell in His home or out in the wilderness alone?

Is there any other place that can provide something as great as what God promises? I believe the answer is no. Just like a child who wants to run away from home in hopes of finding a better place to live, so do we want to escape the pains and frustrations that come along in our dwelling with Christ. But God never promised us Fantasy Land. He promised He would provide, love, teach and guide us. He promised He would set us free. But, included in these promises was the guarantee that there would be rules to live by, demands and a price to pay. Being a Christian can be hard at times, but where else shall we go? If you leave the protection of His presence will you be safe? Or is it possible that you will find yourself alone in the dark—no light to guide you, no provider to feed you, no protector to keep you safe? Will you give up because it is too hard and you are mad, or will you choose to stay at home with Him?

Taking Your Medicine

If you listen carefully to the voice of the Lord your God and do what is right in his eyes, if you pay attention to his commands and keep all his decrees, I will not bring on you any of the diseases I brought on the Egyptians, for I am the Lord, who heals you.
Exodus 15:26

Have you ever . . . tried to get an unwilling child to take some yucky medicine? "Just try it; you'll like it." Or, "This is really good for you; it will make you feel better," are flippant comments we use to convince them to swallow the medicine. But no amount of pleading, bribing or even yelling will get an unwilling child to take unwanted medicine!

I was thinking of this the other day when I was trying to get my child to take some Tylenol to get rid of a 103 degree fever. He was burning up and miserable. He looked so pitiful it made my heart break, and yet as I brought out the medicine, the tears just started to flow uncontrollably. He grabbed his mouth and screamed, "NO!" and I of course felt like the terrible, horrible, mean mommy. But there was one truth I knew—to get rid of the fever meant he had to take the medicine. And as I forced him to take it, I immediately understood how hard and unpleasant it must be for God to have to force us to swallow our medicine too.

What do I mean by our medicine? It is what God brings out of the cabinet when we are sick. It is His remedy to make us well when we are suffering from a particular problem. God's medicine most often means change, especially the change of breaking destructive habits and ways. For me, the medicine is giving up things I love which I know are not good for me—coarse joking, gluttonous eating, pride-filled thoughts. And as I think of God's medicine, I have the same images of shutting my mouth, screaming and opting to stay sick rather than go through the agony of taking that yucky stuff!

Is there a certain habit you know God wants to heal in you? Are you acting like a child holding your mouth and screaming, "No, no! Don't make me! I don't want to!" Before you fight Him any longer, imagine the relief you have when your child finally swallows his medicine. Think of the peaceful healing and rest that begins in their bodies, and then think of yourself as the child who can be healed. God would never try to give you medicine if you didn't need it. He would never just go to that cabinet and give you an unnecessary treatment anymore than you would give a child cough medicine when he was perfectly healthy. God only wants to heal us. So remember His love, His healing powers and how glad you will be when you've finally taken His dose.

"I Hate You!"

Be completely humble and gentle; be patient, bearing with one another in love. Make every effort to keep the unity of the Spirit through the bond of peace. There is one body and one Spirit.
Ephesians 4:2-4
How good and pleasant it is when brothers and sisters live together in unity!
Psalm 133:1

Have you ever... had the opportunity to hear your kids scream "I hate you!" at each other? Unless you are Ozzie and Harriet you have. You never really know how the scuffles get started, but they always seem to escalate quickly. Everyone seems to be getting along and then a subtle argument begins, and before you know it everyone is screaming. "I hate you!" And then another, "I hate you!" And finally, "Well, I hate you more!" In the midst of trying to break them up and help to settle the problem, I find myself burning inside thinking, "What in the world will it take for these guys to get along? What will it take to live in peace and harmony around here?"

The difficult part of being a member of a family is that it does require a concentrated effort to maintain peace. We are not automatically going to get along at all times; rather we, must work at our unity by being considerate, patient and unselfish. As the

Living Bible puts it, we must make "allowances for each other's faults." We must make allowances because, whether we like it or not, whether we want to get along together or not, we all (siblings and parents as well) are still going to be joined together by the bond of our family, so we must make the effort to live at peace.

They say, "You can pick your friends, but you can't pick your family." Well, I've got news for you—as Christians you can't pick your family either. We are all part of one family, with God as our Father. We are brothers and sisters in Christ. We may not like each other all of the time, we may not agree with each other all of the time, but that does not give us the right to scream "I hate you" at our brothers and sisters. Every time we argue with one another saying "I hate you," I guarantee you we are upsetting God in the same fashion we are upset by our kids yelling at one another.

The Bible tells us to love our neighbor as ourselves and to be edifying and encouraging. It doesn't say anything about, "Well, he touched me," or "He crossed on my side." It doesn't say anything about, "She told a lie about me," or "She hurt my feelings." No! It tells us to love one another and to make every effort to "keep the unity." The next time you are ready to say "I hate ... ," remember how upsetting it is as a parent for your children to say they hate one another. Contemplate how displeasing it must be for God to hear His own children say this to each other. And then allow yourself to think of the possibilities in just figuring out a way to get along.

Whom Do You Love Best?

At that time the disciples came to Jesus and asked, "Who is the greatest in the kingdom of heaven?" . . . And he said: "I tell you the truth, unless you change and become like little children, you will never enter the kingdom of heaven. Therefore, whoever humbles himself like this child is the greatest in the kingdom of heaven."
Matthew 18:1-4

Have you ever . . . had a child ask you to pick which child you loved the most? Of course he is sitting ripe and ready to hear his name. He is waiting to proclaim to his siblings, "See, I told you so! I knew she loved me best!" But you, in true, diplomatic, motherly fashion, say, "I love you all the same." How could you ever pick one child over another? You love them equally just because they are yours!

In this passage, the disciples were asking Jesus to pick a favorite by telling them who was going to be the greatest in the kingdom of heaven. Just like little children, they thought if they could claim that name of being the greatest they would reap some heavenly rewards. They were all puffed up and full of pride as they waited with anticipation to hear their own names called. But when the disciples were saying they wanted to be the greatest they were thinking in terms of prizes and rewards, not in terms of self-denial and sufferings. Just as when our children ask who is the most loved, they are looking for special privileges and recognition rather than higher expectations and demands to be placed upon them.

When we become God's children we are promised an inheritance and our inheritance is going to be equal to our brothers' and sisters' in Christ. At the moment of our salvation, we are assured of God's love for us and of our position in eternal life with Him. We don't have to be the greatest to acquire that position. It is a gift and a promise to us as His children. To force God to proclaim whom He loves best then is take His love and make it ugly as it becomes obsessive and possessive.

When we seek to be the greatest it causes us to tear those around us down and to be jealous rather than to build them up in love. Think about the child who wants to be loved the most: will he not pick and tattle on his siblings to make himself look better? That is often what we do as well. We climb over the backs of others, we fail to admit our own flaws, all for the purpose of looking great, all for the purpose of reaping some special favor in the eyes of God and the eyes of those around us. But you are already promised the reward. Won't you live in thanksgiving for yourself as well as for your brothers and sisters too?

Do the Best You Can With the Tools You've Got!

In the church God has appointed first of all apostles, second prophets, third teachers, then workers of miracles, also those having gifts of healing, those able to help others, those with gifts of administration and those speaking in different kinds of tongues. Are all apostles? Are all prophets? Are all teachers? Do all work miracles?
1 Corinthians 12:28-29

Have you ever . . . noticed how affected kids are by peer pressure? "Oh, Claire is unbelievable at tennis. I'll never be that good." Or, "Dan, is the smartest guy in the whole class. I wish I were that smart." They are so busy looking around at the blessings of others they have no appreciation for their own. All they want to be is a clone of the other guy rather than reaching their own potential abilities.

I can remember often as a child comparing myself to others. I'd think, "Oh, if I only had what she had!" And I can always remember my mother saying, "You just have to do the best you can with the tools you've got!" She was wise enough to realize that I would never be the best on the tennis team, nor anywhere close to valedictorian. But she was also smart enough to realize that I didn't have to be these things to be fulfilled. I just had to take what God had blessed me with and use those gifts to the best of my abilities.

I was so busy trying to be someone else I was neglecting who I was supposed to be.

Comparing ourselves to others happens in the body of Christ too. We look around and always seem to see someone other than ourselves who is doing more than we are. But God didn't plan for everyone to be the best on the "team." God knew that everyone could not have the gifts to be apostles, prophets and teachers, but He also knew that others were no less important just because they didn't. In His eyes, everyone was valuable if they used all that He had given them to the best of their ability.

We often look to those who are serving God in different ways from ourselves and wish we could be like them. "I'll never be like them," we think. And that may be true. The good news is we were never designed to be like them. We were designed each with our own special gifts and talents and God expects us to use those the best we can. Quit comparing yourself to whom you deem to be saints all around you. God has a perfect plan and place for you. If He has called you to be a mother, a wife, a friend, be the best that YOU can be. Wherever He has placed you, "do the best you can with the tools you've got!"

The Scroll

A new commandment I
give to you, that you
love one another; as I
have loved you, that you
also love one another.
John 13:34

Have you ever . . . listened to the endless amounts
of things your children hate? You cook something for
dinner—"Oh I hate that!" You say you are going to go
somewhere—"Oh I hate that place!" You say they are
going to have a friend over to play—"Oh I hate him!"
The list of "hates" began growing so quickly in our
home, we had to dub it a four-letter word!

When I was growing up, my mother used to
call my list of hates "The Scroll." Whenever I said I
hated something she would say to get out the Scroll
and put it on the list. She called it this because my list
was so-o-o-o long! I hated everything and everybody!
And what occurs so funny to me now, having
GREATLY reduced my Scroll, is that I never even had
reasons (not legitimate, anyhow) for hating these
things. I just hated them because they were different
from the things I naturally liked.

As a mother now I can see how harmful such
frivolous "hating" can be. God calls us to be loving.
He says to love others as He has loved us. He also
says that we are to love not only the lovable, but the
unlovable as well. This is where the Scroll came into
play. I was loving what I wanted to love and disre-
garding all else. Christ-like love is what separates us

as Christians. It is loving when our natural inclinations are to hate. As one song states, "They will know we are Christians by our love."

How great it would be if every time you met someone you could automatically love them. No prejudged dislikes, just pure love. No saying, "I hate them because: they have gooby hair, they go to G-rated movies, they listen to country music." How great it would be if we could love others as God has loved us. That is His commandment to us. So, as you begin to let this Scripture take root in your heart, think of the people on your Scroll. Then, begin to see them as God sees them—perfect and wonderful! It may seem hard at first, but through the power of the Holy Spirit, you can do it. It may take time but God will surely bless you with love for these people—and anyone else who threatens to be named on your Scroll as well!

Don't Talk About My Child!

Avoid godless chatter, because those who indulge in it will become more and more ungodly.
2 Timothy 2:16

Have you ever . . . had your child have a problem that you were trying to fix and yet still you knew that others were talking about it? The example that comes to my mind was of my oldest child, who, while in preschool, was getting the image of being a bully. He was always pushing and hitting and throwing temper tantrums when he didn't get his way. And I knew there were many kids who did not want to play with him because of that. I knew that other mothers were thinking, and saying, "Why doesn't she get that child under control?" Oh, if it had only been that easy!

We are all so quick to judge and gossip about others problems that we forget to realize how hurtful it really can be. Believe me, I would have loved it if my child had not been acting like that. But he did and I could not just snap my fingers and make it go away. I can still remember how hurtful it was to know how others were talking about him. But my only real course of action was to love him and try to teach him a better way. Ultimately, though, the decision to change would have to come from within him.

How often do we find ourselves gossiping about other people? To us they are just people with juicy tidbits in their lives, but to God these people are

His children. And as a parent who has been hurt by cruel words, I can begin to see how our gossip can be hurtful to God. It's as if He was saying, "Please don't be so unloving. Sure, I know so-and-so is not perfect, but I love him and I am working with him. Don't let this bother you. I am aware and I am in control."

When I think of the people I have gossiped about, I feel bad for not looking at them as God's children and for the hurt that I have caused God when I've done this. I feel bad that I do not have the faith to just love that person and let God be in control. I feel bad because I know the pain that gossip causes because I have experienced that pain myself. We probably all have experienced it, both for our children and ourselves, at one time or another. So next time, rather than gossiping and tearing others down, wouldn't it be wonderful to just love and pray for them, to lift them up and to encourage them through our kindness and trust in God.

The Golden Rule

Do to others what you would have them do to you.

Matthew 7:12

Have you ever . . . asked your child to help pick up a roomful of toys, and gotten the response, "But they're not my toys!"? It doesn't matter to them that they have completely pulled them out of the toy box and have been using them for the past hour. What does matter to them is that the toys are not theirs and thus, they don't have to clean them up. My point is, I don't care whose toys they are, when it is time to clean up everyone helps.

As Christians, we are called to help others in "cleaning up their messes" even if we were not personally responsible for them. We are asked to give money to help the poor. We are asked to be kind to those who are emotionally down. We are asked to do all sorts of things in assisting others when they are in need. It is easy for us to quickly turn away by saying, "It is not my problem," but God calls us to be helpful whether our situation needs help or not. The world is like our children. It says, "Don't bother me. I just want to be left alone and mind my own business. I won't bother you until I need something. And then you better believe I am going to come calling."

"Do to others what you would have them do to you" is also known as the Golden Rule. The world sees it as a feel-good, do-when-you're-in-the-mood type charity. But the Golden Rule is more than just a code of ethics to try and live by. It is our duty as Christians. We don't just help others because it makes us feel good, but because it is a responsibility we carry as children of God. Just as our children must help in carrying out the duties of our own households.

How special is that child who always offers to help clean up toys? They don't moan and groan, they just help. They understand how the family operates as a whole. I help you when you're in need and you help me when I'm in need. I know I didn't cause the mess you are in now, but I know what it is to be helped when I am in need, so I will help you. As Christians, we can no longer be kind to others just when the mood hits. We are called to treat others at all times the way we would have them treat us at all times. So the next time you are asked to help pick up someone else's mess, don't blow them off with an "It's not my problem." Be discerning about how God would have you participate in His family. There could come a time when you will want someone to return the favor!

 Tattletale

> *Why do you look at the speck of sawdust in your brother's eye and pay no attention to the plank in your own eye? . . . You hypocrite, first take the plank out of your own eye, and then you will see clearly to remove the speck from your brother's eye.*
> Matthew 7:3-5

Have you ever . . . had a child tattletale on his brother or sister? "Mom, Billy is watching TV!" or "Mom, Brandon is eating cookies!" Into the room they coming running, ready to spill all about what their "bad" brother or sister is doing. Most of the time I hear them tattle over matters so trivial I really wish they would just save their breath. But tattle they do, because they think in doing so it will bring out the worst in their sibling while making themselves look squeaky clean. It gives the impression they are really good because they have not done this rotten thing, whatever it may be. But we all know, their time will come.

Just as our time will always come. We are all guilty of being the pot who calls the kettle black. I don't think there is one of us who is not guilty of being a tattletale at one time or another. We just can't help ourselves. We are so busy trying to catch others in mistakes that we don't have time to see how we are failing as well. It makes us feel good to think, "Well,

I'm not that bad! At least I don't do that!" But in falling into this trap, we make ourselves judges of others. And we lose sight of the mercy that we have received from God for our own mistakes and should also be giving to others.

Before we are so quick to judge others, God warns us to look at ourselves first. Remember, He tells us, not one is without sin. If we break one of the Commandments, we are guilty of breaking them all. It says in Romans 2:1, "at whatever point you judge the other, you are condemning yourself, because you who pass judgment do the same things." So don't be so harsh on those around you, continually griping about their problems. Try being less of a tattletale and more of an example by worrying about improving the condition of your own heart. As the saying goes, "Don't worry about what they're doing, you just worry about yourself."

Do Your Share

*Freely you have
received, freely give.*
Matthew 10:8

Have you ever . . . had a child who loathed doing household chores? It brings up images in my mind of children lying on the sofa, pleading not to have to clean their rooms or rake the yard or take out the trash. All such menial tasks in the large scope of work that occurs daily in your home, but to them it is monumental. As parents, we look at the situation from the point of view that we have given our children many, many nice things and it's not so much to ask them to do a little work. We hope that they would have some sense of gratefulness, thus causing them to show some appreciation and be willing contributors to work.

But no! Not only do children expect you to give them things, they expect you to do for them too. Their mentality is that they are the children, and thus don't have to work. You are the mom and therefore you do ALL the work. I believe this is not just a problem with present society but has occurred through all generations. Children are by nature lazy and ungrateful. Only as they mature can they realize and appreciate all that is and has been done for them. Only when the shoe is on the other foot, and they become parents, do they finally understand the importance in not only receiving but in giving too.

In the Bible it says that faith without works is dead. We know as Christians that when we are saved by God, it is through faith alone, not by any works of our own. But as we dig deeper, we realize that even though we are not saved by our works, our works reflect how we feel towards the grace God has given us. When we are thankful, we can't help but want to help God with our works. It is not a requirement. It is overflow, something that naturally just spills over from within us.

What is it we have freely received? In our homes, it is the gift of being cared and provided for as we grow up. In Christ's kingdom, it is the gift of eternal life which can never be repaid. So what do we freely give in response to this? In our homes, it is an active participation in doing whatever makes the house function in a clean, efficient, organized manner. In Christ's kingdom, it is contributing in whatever way we can to further God's vision of spreading the Gospel to all. God wants us to freely give of our money, our love, our time and our spiritual gifts—gifts we gladly give to others as a result of acknowledging what He has given to us. The next time you are asked to help a child, a friend or someone within your church, don't be a lazy child moaning on the sofa, "Don't make me do it!" From a heart filled with gratitude, determine to freely give to others in response to all God has freely given you.

Lighten Your Load

Have you ever . . . carried a diaper bag so heavy you thought you would topple over? I mean, when you packed the bag for your "precious new darling," you were determined you would not be caught on the streets in need! You packed bottles, food, diapers, wipes, a change of clothes (or two), blankets, burp pads and toys, all for a 20-minute trip to the grocery store. For me, the fear was that by the time I finally got everything all packed up and ready to go, the baby would be ready to go back to bed for his fourth nap of the day! Anywhere you went, for whatever amount of time, if you had a newborn, it was a major ordeal to leave your house.

But fortunately, as children grow older, the diaper bag begins to lighten. First you stop carrying around extra clothes, then you no longer need to carry bottles, then they outgrow diapers. It was always a huge milestone for me when I could stop using the diaper bag altogether and just stuff my purse with a few necessary items. We could make it from point to point with only an occasional toy and a snack.

As I reflect on Jesus as He called the first disciples to follow Him, I think about how they at once laid their nets and followed him. They did not stop to pack a bag. They did not check to see what they would need. They did not carry anything with them. They just left. They trusted in Jesus so completely to provide for their every need and to handle every situation that might arise that they were not concerned with what they might forget to bring. To lay down their nets, their livelihood, was an acknowledgment of complete trust in Jesus to lead them. Unlike us mothers, who pack our bags to the brim saying, "I will be prepared. No circumstance will arise that I can not handle!", the disciples trusted in Jesus to handle every situation for them.

In reflecting on this passage, I wonder how is it possible to drop everything and follow as they did? It's hard to imagine that a time will come when I will trust Jesus enough to drop all my own concerns and just follow Him. Right now, it seems, there will always be circumstances where I want to be in charge. But what encourages me from the situation of the diaper bag is that a day does come when the bag is lightened and we are able to move about more freely and unencumbered. Little by little, we begin to give those parts of our lives to Christ that previously we held on to just in case we might have a need. And little by little, as we lay down our nets and lighten our loads, we come to realize we have no needs but Him.

Your Pants Are in the Water

> He also said, "This is what the kingdom of God is like. A man scatters seed on the ground. Night and day, whether he sleeps or gets up, the seed sprouts and grows, though he does not know how."
>
> Mark 4:26, 27

Have you ever . . . put a pair of pants on your child only to shriek at how short they had become? You knew you had just bought the pants and now, as if overnight, they were too small! When did he get so tall? You never noticed him growing and yet here he is with "his pants in the water!" With my boys I feel like I return to the store monthly to keep them in clothes that fit. With those gangly long legs growing ever taller, their pants are always in the water! But because I am with them on a day-to-day basis, I can't see the growth occurring

Sometimes I think our Christian walk is that way. We don't really see how we are growing because we are too close to what is happening day to day. It is only as we remove ourselves from our current state of mind and observe where we began and where we currently are that we can see how growth has occurred. For example, as we begin to grow as Christians, we become increasingly more aware of the small sins in our lives. Whereas one day it is natural to look at violence or sex in a movie, as we grow it becomes more and more offensive. I always find myself asking, "When did this happen? I didn't notice any major change in me personally. But I know that this is upsetting to me, whereas before it was not." What is happening is growth. Slowly, but surely, our minds, hearts and actions are becoming more like Christ's. We may not notice it, but the growth is inevitable as we continue to nurture ourselves spiritually.

As parents, we are constantly trying to help our children grow by the nurture and feeding of their bodies. It is only natural through this process that their bodies will grow. And it is the same way for us spiritually. If we feed ourselves by reading the Bible, having fellowship and coming to God in prayer, then our growth is inevitable too.

I am reminded of the classic little boy who wants to be big and strong overnight. He goes around having every one feel his muscles, even though they are small, and then measure him to see how tall he is, even though he is short. He wants so badly to be a grown-up. But it will only happen through time. We need time to grow as well. But one day, to our delight, we go and look in the mirror and we can actually see how we have grown. We can see the change that we've yearned to happen. We may still have a long way to go to become loving, disciplined and pure, but for now we are able to see the sprouts of growth, and for that we can be thankful. For the first time in our lives, others can say, "Your pants are in the water!" and we can smile with joy.

Ma-Ma, Da-Da

This, then, is how you should pray:
Our Father in heaven, hallowed be
your name, your kingdom come,
your will be done on earth as it is
in heaven. Give us today our daily
bread. Forgive us our debts, as we
also have forgiven our debtors.
And lead us not into temptation,
but deliver us from the evil one.
Matthew 6: 9-13

Have you ever . . . jumped for joy when your child spoke his first words? I can still remember the excitement of hearing that first "Ma-Ma" and "Da-Da." I, my husband, the grandparents, all of us were so ecstatic over hearing just those simple words. It wasn't profound, but it was thrilling because it was a beginning. It was the beginning of our being able to communicate with our child.

First words are wonderful because they mark a point where communication can begin. It means your child can communicate her needs in ways beyond falling on the floor crying. It means that she wants to be able to communicate with you. It means it is time to lay the foundation, the model for a whole new language for her.

Prayer is our avenue of communication with God. When we begin as new Christians, we often underestimate the importance of learning how to talk with Him. In our pride, we want to pray the prayers of deeply rooted, mature Christians, and when we can't, we get frustrated, not wanting to pray at all. But we must remember to learn the basics of prayer, just like babies need to learn the basics of speaking a new language.

When Jesus taught the disciples to pray, He began with the basics. He taught the disciples to first praise God, then to ask for forgiveness and finally for protection from temptations and evil. It was His way of saying, "This is Our language. Imitate this so you will be able to communicate with your Heavenly Father." Jesus knew there would be more rejoicing, more applause in heaven over a new Christian saying her first "baby words" than over hearing seasoned Christians praying their prayers. Both are important but it is encouraging to know how thrilling those first words are to God. So if you are one who is afraid to pray, think about that new baby saying those first words. Would you ever want her to stop just because she said "Ba-Ba" instead of "Ma-Ma"? God doesn't want you to stop either. He longs to hear from you and to share in a language that will ultimately bring you closer to Him.

Don't Forget to Eat Your Vegetables

Then Jesus declared, "I am the bread of life. He who comes to me will never go hungry, and he who believes in me will never be thirsty."
John 6:35

Have you ever . . . been exasperated from the thought of having to fix yet another meal for your family? Morning, noon and night you go into the kitchen to prepare something for everyone to eat. Day in and day out you work to bring healthy yet edible meals to everyone in your family. And despite their moaning and groaning of not liking what you cook, you continue on because you know that keeping their bodies nourished is essential. Frankly, it would be a whole lot easier just to let them eat a bag of cookies for dinner rather than spending time preparing and then forcing them to eat a plate full of vegetables. But to allow that would be inviting all kinds of ill health and weak disciplines into their lives.

Sometimes we must do things, not because they are enjoyable, but because we know they are good for us, like when we eat our vegetables. But we need to do more than just feed ourselves with healthy foods to stay healthy. We also must feed ourselves properly with spiritual things. Just as we need to eat vegetables rather than cookies, so we need to spend time being filled up with God and His Word rather than always giving in to our whims like reading books, going to movies or dining out with friends. It is not our natural inclination to want to do this, but we know that it brings great rewards.

It is always so obvious to me when my kids have been eating the wrong foods. If not fed on time they start to get cranky, or if fed the wrong things they become hyperactive and completely out of balance. In the same way, don't you feel yourself get out of balance when you have not been fed in the spiritual discipline of time with God? I know personally I get cranky, impatient, quick tempered and self-gratifying. But as soon as I eat of His bread, I begin to maintain a better balance. I am once again living in a more peaceful, satisfied, contented way.

Jesus wants us to have an appetite for the things he offers. He wants us to partake of Him by reading our Bibles, spending time in prayer and having fellowship with other Christians. These are not always the things we want to do. It doesn't appeal to our taste. But God promises us that as we do these things, we will have good spiritual health. He says we will not be hungry or thirsty. In essence, we will be perfectly filled, nourished and thus energized. The good news is that just because you feed on spiritual things does not always mean you will be eating a plate of broccoli. You will find that spiritual food can be sweet and tasty. You will find that being filled with God is even more satisfying than a plate full of cookies!

When I Grow Up I Want to Be ...

"For I know the plans I have for you," declares the Lord, "plans to prosper you and not to harm you, plans to give you hope and a future."
Jeremiah 29:11

Have you ever... talked with your child about what she wants to be when she grows up? One of my boys always says he wants to be a policeman, while the other one wants to be a fireman. Of course, they are still in preschool, so it is impossible to know what their final destiny will be but what I find important in discussing with them their dreams and goals is that they begin to see a vision of the future. They begin to see and comprehend that all of the work that they are doing, even in their young lives, is a training ground for something that they will one day become.

As parents, we are never certain about the destinations of our children. But what we do is continually try to guide them into activities where we believe they will prosper. For example, my oldest son has a natural gift of gab. He loves to talk to people and is very curious. I believe he will make an outstanding salesman. So, in preparation for his future, I know I will try to guide him into activities that will promote these skills. In encouraging him to use his gift, I hope he will find a future that will be greatly rewarding to him. And as I guide him, I never give up hope that something great is going to happen to him.

God knows that there is a great future in store for us as well. Just like our children, that destination is unknown. But we are assured that if we develop our skills and follow His guidance, our futures will be rewarding. The King James version says that God will give us an "expected end." What do you think that expected end will be? I believe it will be simply a place of peace, joy and contentment. That is our planned destiny, our future and our hope. But as the Amplified Bible states, our hope is in our "final" outcome. And so it is we will not find this place of peace until the end of our lives.

I write this because I believe that as we get older, we give up on our futures. Often we see them as bleak, feeling as if there is no time left to have prosperous, joyful destinations. But time is of no essence to God. He sees the time for us to succeed just as we see the great amount of time for our own children to succeed. He always has something wonderful in store for us. His hope for us is not the present but the future. His plans are a continual work in progress. So spend some time talking with God about your future. He will set dreams in your head and then guide you along the path to discover them!

Hot Stoves

I do not understand what I do. For what I want to do I do not do, but what I hate I do.
Romans 7:15

Stop doing wrong, learn to do right!
Isaiah 1:16

Have you ever . . . gotten mad at a child because she has repeatedly done something you have asked her not to do? I envision the numerous times I have asked my kids not to go near a hot stove. But what do they do? Like a magnet, they immediately go near the hot stove. I can hear myself warning them, "Don't go near the stove, it's hot." Then again more emphatically, "Don't go near the stove, it's hot!!" Finally, in a panic, screaming, "DON'T GO NEAR THE STOVE, IT'S HOT!!!" No matter what kind of warnings I give, I can't seem to get my kids to do what I say. It is one thing for them to know that the stove is hot and quite another thing for them actually not to touch it!

But don't we all put our hand on the "hot stove" even though we know it will hurt us? I can't even count the times when I know God has told me not to do things and yet I go and do the very thing He has said not to do. "Do not complain. Do not gossip. Do not be proud. Do not argue. Do not envy. Do not hate. Do not love yourself over others." And what do I do? Complain, gossip, argue and hate—exactly what He has said not to do. It's not as if God's laws are a mystery to me any more than my rules for my kids are a mystery to them. It is simply a matter of being wise enough to choose one will over the other—God's or our own. Will we be like our children and pick our own will, putting ourselves into danger, or will we choose to do what God says and keep ourselves safe?

At what point will we become mature enough to take the knowledge that God gives us and translate that into action? How do we bring our beliefs into convictions where, no matter what, we will do what we know to be right? It is only as we become strengthened in our knowledge that we will begin to become wise enough to choose God's will over our own. Just as our own children must mature and begin to do the right things, so must we eventually begin to make wiser choices. We cannot remain newborn babies forever. It makes me sad and embarrassed to think about a grown adult who still acts foolish like a child, but no more than when I think about a Christian who still foolishly behaves like the day he first accepted Christ. We must learn to "stop doing wrong and learn to do what is right!"

Red Rover, Red Rover

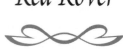

> Put on the full armor of God so that you can take your stand against the devil's schemes.
>
> Ephesians 6:11

Have you ever . . . played the game of "Red Rover"? You know the game where two teams line up holding hands. One team yells, "Red Rover, Red Rover, send 'so-and-so' right over," and that person comes charging across the yard to try and break through the gripped hands of the opposing team. If 'so-and-so' is successful, he gets to pick someone from the line he has just broken through to come back and be on his team, but if unsuccessful, he has to join the other team.

Of course the game of "Red Rover" is a game of strength, strength to overpower the enemy. But what I remember most are the feelings of being weak. I was never fully confident that I was strong enough to overpower the other team. So when I heard them calling, "Red Rover, Red Rover send Margaret right over," my stomach would sink worrying that they had called my name. I imagined that if the opposing team called my name, they would in essence be announcing to everyone that they thought I was a weakling. As they called my name, they were in essence saying, "We want you to send Margaret right over. We know she is a weakling and she'll never be able to break through our line!"

And as if that wasn't bad enough as a child, I often feel like I am still caught up playing the game of "Red Rover" as an adult—only now it is in the game of life and my opponent, instead of being the girls in the neighborhood, is none other than the devil himself. In the midst of every battle and temptation I face in life, I can hear the devil personally shouting, "Red Rover, Red Rover send Margaret right over." And then I can hear the chuckle of the devil and his team murmuring, "Watch this. There is no way she'll ever be able to conquer this battle."

But at this point all of us can learn from the game of "Red Rover" that the game of life is really no game at all, but rather a spiritual battleground. Because it is in this life that the devil is constantly trying to force us to join his side. Just as kids in the game of "Red Rover" call the names of the weaklings, so the devil uses the same strategy. He tries to bully us into believing we are too weak to overcome him. He tries to make us fearful that he will call our names to stand up against him, thus showing to everyone how weak we are.

But we must not forget that if we are on Jesus' "team," we are never too weak to fight the devil. We are never too weak because we are provided with the "full armor of God" that is offered to us in this Scripture. No matter what battles come our way—dealing with addictions, traumas, or character flaws—we are always stronger than the devil because we are made strong through God. We must be sure to put this armor on every day. Satan loves nothing more than to catch us by surprise, when we are feeling overconfident and assured of our victory. It is only by constantly being alert to his tactics that we will survive—and maybe even be able to bring someone else back to our team!

Life Is Like an Ice Cream Cone

For this very reason, make every effort to add to your faith, goodness; and to goodness, knowledge; and to knowledge, self-control; and to self-control, perseverance; and to perseverance, godliness; and to godliness, brotherly kindness; and to brotherly kindness; love. For if you possess these qualities in increasing measure, they will keep you from being ineffective and unproductive in your knowledge of our Lord, Jesus Christ.
2 Peter 1:5-8

Have you ever . . . watched a child eating an ice cream cone? It is a true art trying to keep the ice cream from running down his hand. It requires complete concentration to ensure that one side doesn't melt before another. A little lick on one side fixes the first drip, but then the other side will start to melt. So the child quickly licks on that side until the other side begins to drip again—and on and on it goes.

Often I feel like my life resembles the balancing act of the ice cream cone. Little by little, I work on areas of my life to get them under control. I will see an area, like self-control, that begins to falter, so I begin to work on that part. But as soon as I put my focus on self-control, I notice that another area, like love, begins to have problems and I must redirect my attention to put more love into my life. And then, just like the ice cream cone, I continually work around all the qualities of my life to keep them under control.

It is a reality, even though a difficult one, that we are able to keep our lives together only by being attentive to many things at once. But the good news, as Peter tells us in this scripture, is that we are to expect to work on many things at once. And if we are to expect it, then we know that God will be the one to help us to keep all these areas of our lives in balance as well as to increase them in good measure.

It is only by allowing God to work in our lives, inch by inch, "lick by lick," that we are able to "possess these qualities in increasing measure." As we allow Him to work on goodness in our lives, we also begin to let Him increase our knowledge, and then He moves us over to build self-control. It doesn't happen all at once. God is gradually, but collectively, working on many aspects of our character at the same time. He helps us with our balance as we apply these lessons so that we may live fruitful, productive lives. If you feel your life can become out of control at times, remember to allow God to help you with your balance. He will help you to grow in these qualities. He will help you to keep the "ice cream drips" of life from becoming out of control!

Dropping the Popcorn

> "But mark this: There will be terrible times in the last days. People will be lovers of themselves, lovers of money, boastful, proud, abusive, disobedient to their parents, ungrateful, unholy, without love, unforgiving, slanderous, without self-control, brutal, not lovers of the good, treacherous, rash, conceited, lovers of pleasure rather than lovers of God—having a form of godliness but denying its power. Have nothing to do with them.
>
> 2 Timothy 3:1-5

Have you ever . . . tried to keep your child from seeing something violent or "dirty"? My mom always referred to this as "Dropping the Popcorn!" Whenever we would go to the movies and a scene of questionable taste would come on the screen she would act like she dropped the popcorn and then would ask my brothers and me to lean forward and clean up the mess, thus avoiding temporarily what was on the screen. We, of course, had no clue we were missing something "dirty" and would resume our positions sitting up in our chairs when it was over.

As parents, we do our best to protect our children from the evil ways of the world. We don't want them to witness violence and sex or to hear profanity. We monitor everything to the best of our abilities, but it is a constant challenge because sometimes it just seems as if evil is lurking everywhere. And it is so tempting just to take a peek. Children, just as adults, want to see what the forbidden fruit is all about. But one peek is all the devil needs to take major control in our lives.

Satan is constantly trying to lure us all in to lustful thoughts, gossip, the love of money, the love of pleasure. We all think we can have just a taste and then we can turn away. But God knows how hard it is to turn away, so we are warned, have NOTHING to do with these. Not even a peek!

The best answer is just to "drop the popcorn," to not even let our eyes witness what we know is not good for us, to turn the channel so to speak. As you become conscious of the ways in which you can protect your children from certain T.V. shows, certain people, certain places, also be aware of how God tries to protect us. He advises us through His Word what to avoid. He tells us not even to look at that which is harmful. The less we have of Satan in our eyes, our hearts and our minds the better! So the next time the devil tries to get a foothold in your life, drop the popcorn! Run, flee, do whatever you can, but don't allow his wickedness in your life.

The Apple Doesn't Fall Far from the Tree

You call me "Teacher" and "Lord," and rightly so, for that is what I am. Now that I, your Lord and Teacher, have washed your feet, you also should wash one another's feet. I have set you an example that you should do as I have done for you.
John 13:13-15

Have you ever . . . noticed how children tend to follow in their parents' footsteps? Whatever role is modeled for them is what they usually become. Good character by the parents, good character by the child. Bad character by the parents, bad character by the child. And now, as a parent, I can see and appreciate the sacrifices and disciplines my parents made in order to be role models for me.

It's funny how I find myself constantly calling my mother now and thanking her for the things she did for me, because finally I realize how hard it was. Whereas once I took for granted all that she did to model what she wanted me to become, the tides have now turned as I come to understand her sacrifice through copying her and doing the same for my children. Enduring the endless whining, the barking of orders for food and drinks, the getting up in the middle of the night, the helping with homework and carpooling are all a part of the way she showed me what it means to love as well as what it means to serve. She was the example to me so that I would later know how to be with my children.

In order to help someone learn, you must be an example for them in the things you are trying to teach. When Jesus got on His knees at the Last Supper and washed the disciples' feet, it was one of His most poignant moments as an example of servanthood—of teaching us by example how He wanted us to behave and what He wanted us to become. It was the bowing down to Himself so that others could see the importance of bowing down to themselves. Jesus knew how important it is to practice what you preach and He lived a life exactly as He wanted us to live. He knew that, just as children, our minds are like sponges. They absorb everything going on around us and they emulate what they see. It is only natural. If they see love, service and good morals, they will mimic this. But if they see laziness, gossip and hatred, it too will reap its harvest.

How are you doing as an example to those around you—especially your children? Are you asking them to do things you are not doing yourself? Remember the apple doesn't fall far from the tree. Your actions will speak louder than any words ever could. Be as Christ and emulate those traits which you want others to possess.

Follow the Leader

> Be imitators of God, there-
> fore, as dearly loved children
> and live a life of love, just as
> Christ loved us and gave
> himself up for us as a fra-
> grant offering and sacrifice
> to God.
> Ephesians 5:1,2

Have you ever . . . watched your children playing Follow the Leader? You can just imagine a line of boys and girls jumping, hopping, rubbing their heads, poking their noses, doing somersaults and bouncing in the air to do jumping jacks. The leader is the head of the game, the one to create all the moves that everyone else must follow. Whatever the leader does, the rest of the group must copy exactly or they are out!

I believe our life is like a continuous game of Follow the Leader. And who is our constant leader? Jesus, of course! Everything He has done we are to copy. He forgives, we forgive. He loves the unlovable, we love the unlovable. He puts himself last and becomes a servant, we put ourselves last and become a servant. He gives to others of himself, we give to others of ourselves. Whatever Jesus did during His life was the perfect example for us as we follow and live our lives.

The game of Follow the Leader always makes me giggle. It is so much fun to see the outrageous acts the leader expects everyone to perform. And I can just hear the kids playing when someone challenges the leader, "You want me to do what?" They know it is crazy and absurd but so much fun to actually do the outrageous. Well, what better game can we play in life than to follow the One who will cause this same joy in our lives? When we follow Christ, He will make us giggle at the unbelievable things He also expects us to do. But as we follow Him, we come to see how the impossible becomes the possible!

Everyone knows that in Follow the Leader if you don't follow, you lose. And it is the same for us as we follow Jesus. If you don't follow, you lose! You lose because you miss out on the joy He is ready to give to you. But if you do follow, if you copy every move He made, you will lead a life full of joy. You will find yourself doing the unexpected, the unimaginable, as you imitate Him. If He did it, we know that we will be able to do it too. How are you doing at this game? Are you winning or are you losing? It is never too late to play. You can always begin to follow Christ and He will lead you in a game full of life, full of joy and full of doing the unimaginable!

The Battle of the "I Wants"

Keep your lives free from the love of money and be content with what you have.

Hebrews 13:5

Have you ever . . . been overwhelmed by all of the "stuff" your kids want you to get for them? It is a never ending battle of the "I-wants." Check-out lines at the grocery stores are exasperating as the kids beg for every last thing they see. T.V. commercials lure them to want toy after toy after toy. Going over to play at friends' houses causes them to see what toys and games other people have and yearn for those. Whatever they don't have, they want and that which they do have, they want more of. It is an insatiable appetite to see and then to want. I can easily get mad at my children when they are so ungrateful. And it breaks my heart that they can be so unappreciative for all of the things that they have been given. But I can certainly understand my children's ways.

Have we not all been guilty of wanting more, of being discontent with our present "things"? How many times have you had the "I-wants" when you wanted someone else's home, their job, their clothes, a personality trait, or even just their figure? Just as I look at my child's room and feel disgusted by the excess of toys, so I can look at my own room and see the closet full of clothes, the drawer full of jewelry, the room full of books and knickknacks, and on and on and on, and wonder how can I still desire more? How can I still want more when I hardly have room nor do I appreciate half of that which I already have?

We've all been fooled by the world's claims that to have and to own brings contentment, that our next purchase will be the one to still our hearts, give us joy, cause us to want no more. To think if only I had that!! But the things of this world do not bring satisfaction, because the world believes that nothing is ever enough. There is always something more, something better just around the corner. It is only when we look to Christ that we can "be content with what we have."

As a parent, we can see how unhealthy it is for a child to not be content. It causes jealousy, bitterness, unkind words and anger when wants are not met. And it causes children to be continually focused on themselves and thinking of their own desires and never the cares of others. We all look at our kids and say "How could you possibly want more? You should be so thankful, so overjoyed for everything you've been given!" My gosh, why do we think it is any different for us as adults? How often do you think the Lord looks upon us and says those exact words? "Look at all you have and yet still you lust for more. Be content with what you have." It is hard not to want what the world wants and yet our peace comes from being content in all we have through Christ.

Eyes in the Back of My Head

> Nothing in all creation is hidden from God's sight.
> Hebrews 4:13
>
> Where can I go from your Spirit? Where can I flee from your presence?
> Psalm 139:7

Have you ever . . . told your child you have "eyes in the back of your head?" I always tell my kids this when they ask how I knew something they did—which they thought they'd done in secret. And I was never so successful as when I'd say this when we were riding in our car.

Thanks to some wonderful inventor, I have a small magnified mirror that rests on my sun visor. This mirror allows me to see quite clearly everything that is going on in the seats behind me. When my children provoke each other, unbuckle their seat belts to crawl around the car, spill food and do other things they shouldn't, they're caught! I never even turn my head to look back! This unbelievable foresight of mine always causes them to scream, "How did you know we did that?" EYES IN THE BACK OF MY HEAD.

Truthfully, it is just a matter of watching my kids closely, even when they are unaware of it. Whether they like it or not, whether they realize it or not, I am always keeping tabs on their activities, for their sake as well as mine! I want to know what they are up to so that the moment they go off by themselves, get really quiet and start being "up to no good," I am there to get them back in line where they should be.

It is the same when we are up to no good. God has those ever present parental "eyes in the back of His head." We think we can get away with something by sneaking off alone and doing whatever it is that gets us into trouble—things like breaking wedding vows, lying about how we're spending our money, eating more than we know is healthy for us. We think, "No one will ever know. I can get away with this." But then, we get caught, because God always knows. There is nothing hidden from His sight. You may think that because no one is physically watching, your behavior is going undetected, but God is an ever-present God. He is with us everywhere we go and He knows everything we are doing. That is why it is so important that we are consistent in who we are. The character and integrity we present to the world is the same character as when we are by ourselves.

So the next time you want to do something wrong, remember how you always know what your children are up to as a loving parent should. Whether you like it or not, God knows everything about you. Don't resent His presence, rather do everything with integrity knowing that He has His eye on you.

What Will It Take to Satisfy You?

But godliness with contentment is great gain. For we brought nothing into the world, and we can take nothing out of it. But if we have food and clothing, we will be content with that.
1 Timothy 6:6-8

Have you ever . . . had a child that just could not be satisfied? If you give him one of something, he wants two. If you give him five, he wants 10. No matter what he receives, it is never enough! Whether it is candy, toys or even affection, nothing is ever enough. The child just cannot be pleased. He always sees his cup as half empty, never looking at what he has received, instead focusing on what he has not received. I have a child like this and his discontentment always leaves me in frustration, asking the question, "What will it take to satisfy you? At what point is enough enough?"

Do you think God might ever have reason to ask you that same question? What will it take to satisfy you? Will you be satisfied with one child, or does it have to be more? Will you be satisfied as being a mom, or do you have to have a career too? Will you be satisfied having only God's love, or do you have to stretch yourself thin so you will have all the love and approval of others, too? What will it take to make you completely satisfied?

I always felt this was an important question to ask my child when he began his "Poor me, I never get a thing" attitude. It allowed him to see that the things he begged for would never have a limit. Nothing was ever going to be enough. By asking this question, I could let him see that contentment comes from within and not from "things." Contentment is a mind set, an attitude. It is a sense of inward sufficiency and peace. When you stop to ask, "What it will take to satisfy you?" then you realize nothing is ever enough.

So why not try a different route? Why not stop the dog and pony show of trying to please your child or of trying to please yourself and discover the true path to contentment? It is not from things, but rather, as Paul says, through Christ. The path to being truly rich is not through material possessions but through our inner joy that comes from being connected to Christ. When we look for satisfaction in the world, we will always seek more and receive less. It is only when we look to Christ that we can be truly contented. The gifts He gives us are the ones that fill us up, make us whole, complete and satisfied. The gift of the Holy Spirit, the gift of His Word, the gift of love, the gift of Himself. What will it take to satisfy you? The answer is Him!

Think About Something Else

When an evil spirit comes out of a man, it goes through arid places seeking rest and does not find it. Then it says, "I will return to the house I left. When it arrives, it finds the house unoccupied, swept clean and put in order. Then it goes and takes with it seven other spirits more wicked than itself, and they go in and live there. And the final condition of that man is worse than the first.

Matthew 12:43-45

Have you ever . . . had a time when your children drove you crazy with misdirected thinking? Some of my favorite examples are: just before dinner when they start nagging you about letting them eat a bag of cookies. Or near their birthday when they dream about a pricey gift they think they deserve and continuously beg you to give to them. Or when they are bored and can't stop asking you to drive them to a friend's house while you are stuck at home waiting on a repair man. Their minds are focused on the wrong things and, like a pit bull, they won't let those thoughts go.

It is times like these when I say, "Just think about something else." But we all know how hard that can actually be. It is difficult to try and remove a thought, and even harder to refill our minds with something of worth rather than just another bad thought. But, as we learn in these scriptures, in order to have a peaceful condition in our minds, we must learn to "transform and renew" our minds when they get off track. It is similar to how we use the remote control to change the T.V. One minute we can be totally engrossed in a soap opera but as soon as the channel is changed, say to the news, we forget about the soap opera, and become involved in the news. By simply putting another image in our minds, they have instantly been transformed.

But have you ever noticed how hard it is to change your kid's persistent thoughts patterns? They don't easily give up those "bad" thoughts. Our responsibility as parents is to reeducate and redirect their thoughts when they are off-center. Instead of telling them not to think about the bag full of cookies, we must keep their minds filled in other, more fruitful ways.

Just as parents help redirect their children's thoughts, the Holy Spirit is the one who helps us redirect ours. He first convicts us of our wrong thinking and then helps us to "renew" our minds by thinking about what God would have us thinking. Remember, the mind is very powerful. We must continually be aware of who is controlling our thoughts—God or the world. We must be sure we continually keep our thought patterns under His control. It is a scary thing to leave our minds open and free for Satan to come in with his seven ugly spirits and destroy the good work that God has created in us. To avoid this, we must keep our minds continually transformed, renewed and centered on the things of God. Listen to the Spirit when He tells you to "just think about something else." Be willing to "flick the channel changer" of your mind. As you do, you will come to understand what it is to be blameless, pure and full of peace.

Mommies Know Everything

O Lord, you have searched me and you know me. You know when I sit and when I rise; you perceive my thoughts from afar.

Psalm 139:1-2

Have you ever . . . had your child ask you for something and you knew what the request would be before he ever even opened his mouth? A perfect example of this is when my kids were toddlers and would come into the kitchen for what I felt was the 100th cup of juice of the day. They would toddle in with their empty sippy cups and their pitiful little faces and I immediately knew their need. I had sensed this need so many times I began to wonder if I was becoming a juice-pouring robot. So before they started with their pleading I would say, "Stop right there! You don't even have to ask. I know what you want."

How did I know what they wanted? Well because Mommies know everything of course! Actually, though, it was through personal experience with my kids. I have seen them grow from the very first days of their lives. I have watched their habits, their personalities and behaviors. I know everything about them because I have watched them "sit and rise" and have made it my goal to be aware of all that happens in their lives (at least for now).

But one day I realized how in tune God is to our lives, just as we are to our children's lives. This particular day I was facing a problem that was causing me a lot of anxiety. After days of sporadic prayer, I decided to sit down and completely focus my time on pleading to God for answers about this situation. No sooner had I sat down to plead and beg for answers when I heard God say, "Stop right there! I have heard you ask me for this. I know your needs. I know them so much better than you do." He also added, "I will answer you, but you must believe that I know you and you must be patient." That was it. As I heard this I began to dwell on how well God does know us. He knows every thought and every need—everything! I didn't have to be anxious about pleading to God because He already knew what I needed.

When my kids were asking me to pour juice for them, I knew their need and I wanted them to know that I knew. But I also wanted them to have patience while I fulfilled those needs. What God was saying is He wants us to know He knows our needs and to ask us to be patient in fulfilling them as well. God is omniscient. He has complete understanding and insight into our lives and He loves us infinitely. When we ask of God through prayer, we must be confident of His knowledge of us. We must be confident that He always hears our needs and will fulfill the desires of our hearts. We must be confident that He knows everything!

Fears in the Night

He shall call upon me, and I will answer him; I will be with him in trouble.
Psalm 91:15

I will never leave you nor forsake you.
Joshua 1:5

The Lord is near.
Philippians 4:5

Have you ever . . . had your child loudly and suddenly call your name in the middle of the night? You were dead asleep and out of nowhere came a bloodcurdling "Mommy!" What did you do? You jumped up immediately and ran to that child's side. It didn't matter that you had no clue what hour it was or that you couldn't even figure out where you were because you were so startled. What was important was that your child was calling and because you loved him you would come running to see what was the matter and how you could help.

Did you ever consider that God always comes running when we call on Him? It doesn't matter what time of day or where we are, He hears us and comes running. He is never too tired or too busy with something else. God always answers. And when He does, He comforts our fears. Just like children, our fears and troubles can be real or imaginary, but God helps us to overcome both. He helps us handle the problems that are real by comforting us with His presence and offering solutions to the problems. For our problems that are imaginary, He alters our way of thinking so we are able to overcome the false fears and anxieties.

Have you ever wondered if God will come to your side when you are scared in the night? Do not ever be fooled into thinking that He will not answer. He is a more loving parent than you or I could ever dream to be, and He is always faithful to His promises. God promises that He will answer us when we call on Him in times of trouble, that He will never leave us nor forsake us and He promises that He is always near. You can be assured that just as you would not leave a child screaming in the night, more so would He not leave you. He can come from the highest places in heaven to the lowest places of darkness in an instant. Do not lose your hope and your joy due to your fears. God will always rush to His children's side when they call to Him in the dark.

Can I Please Have Something to Drink?

God is not a man, that he should lie, nor a son of man, that he should change his mind. Does he speak and then not act? Does he promise and not fulfill?
Numbers 23:19

Have you ever . . . told your child you would do something for him just to get him off your back? What comes to my mind is the bedtime ritual when my child screams through the door for that one last cup of something to drink before he will go to sleep. I am usually completely exhausted, having told all of the stories I can tell, and as I leave the room, thinking I have finally gotten him to bed, he yells out, "Can I please have something to drink?" As I groan at the thought of having to do one more thing, I flippantly say to him, "Sure, I'll bring you something in just a minute." But when I say this, I am never 100 percent committed to bringing that last drink. My secret wish is that after I leave the room, they will quickly fall asleep, thereby avoiding that last little chore for me to do.

One night, however, a problem arose in my system. I made this promise to my child, my husband heard it and then he watched me as I curled up on the sofa with my book once I had gotten downstairs. He could not believe that I had made a promise to our son and then not followed through. He made the comment to me that that child would be waiting on me.

Even if he fell asleep, he would remember the next day that I had not come up with his drink. It did not matter that I said it knowing he would probably be fast asleep. What counted was that a promise was a promise. As long as that child was under my care, he would be observing whether I was faithful or not in fulfilling my promises. Well, I can tell you that my husband caught my attention and I no longer tell my children something just to appease them in hopes it will get them off my back. I have visions of them waiting for me to follow through on promises, only to find a mother who can't keep her word.

No person on earth has kept every promise he's ever made, except one—Jesus! It says in this verse, "Does he promise and not fulfill?" Did you know that God cannot and will not make a promise or a commitment to you, and then let you down? What He commits to in His Word is what you can believe will be true. Have you taken the time to read Scripture to know what God's promises are to you, and do you know that He will always follow through? He does not give us every whim and fancy that we ask for, but He absolutely keeps every promise He makes to us. Some of those include: His unfailing love, His complete forgiveness, His unending comfort, His absolute wisdom. The list goes on as you search the Bible. Remember as you wait for Him, God is constant and faithful. He will always fulfill His Word. He will never leave you longing for "a drink in the night!"

The Clinging Leg Syndrome

My God is my rock, in whom I take refuge.

Psalm 18:2

Be strong and courageous. Do not be afraid or terrified because of them, for the Lord your God goes with you; he will never leave you nor forsake you.

Deuteronomy 31:6

Have you ever . . . tried to leave a young child in an unfamiliar environment? Whenever I took one of my children to Sunday School or to a new friend's house to play, I can remember him clinging frantically to my leg in fear. "No-o-o-o," he would scream, "I don't want to go. Don't leave me, please." And gently, but forcefully, I would try to loosen the death grip around my leg. Although he was hysterical with fear, being in this unknown situation, I knew that I would never leave them some place unsafe. I knew that everything would be all right.

But I could completely sympathize with his emotions. It is scary to be in unknown environments. Plenty of questions pop in his mind like, "Who will I know? What will we be doing? Am I going to be safe? Will my mommy be coming back?" Of course, I always knew all of the answers, so I was secure about leaving him. But even though I was confident, it was important that I relay that confidence to him. "Daniel and Peter will be here. You will play for awhile and then bake some cookies. Peter's mommy will be there if you need anything, and I will be back to get you in one hour." My words and their trust in me had to be worthy enough to give him courage to let go of my leg.

But don't we all feel that same urge to cling ferociously to someone or something when left in an unfamiliar environment? Whether it is stepping out on a limb to lead a Bible study or to face the loss of someone important in our life or to overcome personal battles of addiction or bad habits, we want someone to convince us that everything is going to be all right. We want someone to tell us just as we would tell our child, "You are going to teach this Bible Study for 10 weeks. Sally, Mary, Joan and Beth will be there. There will be lots of fun discussion, you will learn a lot and you will be sadder when it is over than you are fearful now."

But what is so great about God is He does give us those words so we can let go of our fear. Although He doesn't give us every specific, He absolutely speaks to our hearts to calm our individual needs. And when He promises us we will be safe, then we can be assured we will be safe. We've got to trust Him, just as we ask our kids to trust us. But that trust comes only little by little as we experience more and more of the fulfillment of those promises.

Do you believe in God's words enough to take refuge in Him? Know that He will never leave you anywhere that is unsafe. If you are fearful, ask your questions, but believe in His answers. If you find yourself fearing the environment where He has left you, know that God is coming back to get you. Be a big boy or girl. Be strong and courageous. Let go of your fears, anxieties and worries and take refuge in Him.

1 Want to Go Home

If you make the Most High your dwelling—even the Lord, who is my refuge—then no harm will befall you, no disaster will come near your tent.

Psalm 91:9-10

Have you ever... had a friend of your child's spend the night and at midnight, they cry out, "I want to go home!"? You can feel that sense of dread coming over you as you try to calm her fears. Not only do you not want her upset, but you also don't want to have to call her parents at midnight to say their child is coming home. But there is just something about that midnight hour, when we realize that we are all alone in the dark, when we all want scream out, "I want to go home!"

What is it about home that we yearn for? Home is safety. Home is our protection from danger. It is familiar and safe. It is a place where you know your parents will take care of everything. It is a place where you know you will find solutions, comfort, and love. Home is the place where we can be completely ourselves. We are loved and accepted as who we are, no strings attached.

Often I know exactly what that child at midnight is feeling. When I am tired, scared, uncertain of what is to come, I can hear myself whisper, "I just want to go home." And even though I always have my physical home, which is definitely my place of safety, it is not always possible for me to make it there when I am in need. So where can we go when we can't make it home? We go to God, the "Most High," and make Him our dwelling, our habitation, our home. As they say, "Home is where your heart is." Wherever I may be, I always know if I turn to God, no harm will befall me. He is my safety, my comfort, the place where I can be myself. When I call to Him in prayer, I am home. He comes and picks me up, so to speak, no matter what the hour, and He doesn't ever mind being woken up. He is always ready to pull all of us back under His wing and protect us, to give us rest and let us know we are safe with Him. When you become scared in the night, or at any other time, call to Him and say you want to come home. He will be there in an instant!

I Just Want to Be with You

Come near to God
and he will come
near to you.

James 4:8

Have you ever . . . felt like your child came to you only when she needed something? She knew that you could give her money, or food, or a ride somewhere, or advice, or something else of value. But other than that, you were pretty much a non-entity. She was content to let you do for her, but as far as building a relationship and spending time together, she would just as soon not bother.

But did you ever consider that our children don't spend time with us because they don't understand we yearn to have more of a relationship with them than just being the provider and disciplinarian? I think it is hard for my kids to believe that I would rather hear about how their day went at school than talk to my friends on the phone. I do want to share in their day-to-day lives. I want a bond to develop between us. I want them to see me as someone they can share all their experiences of life with as well as someone they look to for guidance and provisions.

Just as children find it hard to believe that parents want to spend time with them, I believe many of us find it hard to believe that God wants to spend time with each of us too. We see Him as the distant parent ready on alert to handle our needs. We make emergency 911 calls to Him only when we can't handle things ourselves. But as far as spending time with Him goes, we don't bother. We think He has other things to do.

But God does care about our day-to-day activities, our joys, our hurts, our frustrations, our victories. He yearns for us to come to Him and divulge it all. He wants us to talk about the fight with our friend, how bad we feel while we're pregnant, how nice our boss was to us—everything! He already knows what is happening in our lives, but He revels in the time He gets to spend with each of His precious children.

We all know what it is like to call on someone who never calls us back, or to have someone only come to us when they need something. It is not much fun. You feel used. You would much rather that your relationships be two-way-streets with each person giving as well as receiving. So make your relationship with God a two-way street as well. Don't just call on Him when you are in need. Spend time just getting to know Him. Discover who He is, how fabulous, merciful and loving He is. Give to Him and share of yourself as you would with others who are important to you. Then you will find the dearest friendship you will ever know. I promise! As you draw near to Him, He will draw near to you.

The Harasser

Jesus Christ is the
same yesterday and
today and forever.
Hebrews 13:8

Have you ever . . . had a child harass you for something he wanted? Not all children will do this. I have one child who accepts No as an answer and he leaves an issue alone. But I have another child whom our family has appropriately nicknamed "the harasser." On every single issue, he presses and presses until eventually he gets his way. He'll ask, "Mom can I have a snack?" even though I am minutes away from putting dinner on the table. Or he'll ask, "Mom can I go outside and play?" even though it is 20 degrees and raining outside. He knows what the answer is going to be when he asks but he is ready for my No and then he begins the harassing, the Chinese water torture of asking the same question over and over until finally I crack down and agree to his request. "Yes. Sure. Fine. Do it. Just quit harassing me!" I hate to crack, to give in. It infuriates me, but he just beats me down.

The good news is, though, that where I am so weak as a parent, God is so strong. He is so good and so steadfast. He is like an immovable rock that can't be changed or bribed or persuaded when we harass him for things that are not good for us. A case in point. My eating habits are an area that have often caused me to worry unnecessarily. I have begged and pleaded and harassed God for so many years to just change my whole way of thinking about food. I have lazily tried to take an easy way out by trying to exercise more without changing my poor eating habits. But try as I might, God would never budge. Giving in to a life of gluttonous eating was not good for me and He would not allow me to have my way when my way was the wrong way. But as I look back over the years to see how I am finally overcoming my bad habits, I am so thankful that God did not crack.

If He had given in to my pleas, like I do with my children, I would never have had the peace that I have now. I wouldn't be strong or know that I could overcome. I wouldn't have the discipline to do the right thing even though I so desired to do the "wrong" thing. I am thankful that God is never changing. He is the same yesterday, today and forever. He can not be swayed with the wind like we can be. His truths are set in stone and as much as we plead, they do not alter. So when you come to Him "harassing" for that which is not good for you, remember He is like a rock, immovable and strong. The only thing that He will allow to be changed in your situation is the way your mind changes to think like His.

Take the Plunge

Now faith is being sure of what we hope for and certain of what we do not see.

Hebrews 11:1

Have you ever... tried to lure a frightened child into jumping into a pool? I can remember when both of my children were first learning to swim, afraid to jump in the pool. They would stand on the side, toes on the edge, wanting so much to jump, but just not being able to. Meanwhile, I was in the water splashing and coaxing them to come in. "Just jump! The water feels great! You will love it!" But as much as they wanted to jump, they were frozen on the cement, missing all of the fun.

Deep inside them, their faith was being tested. They believed that I was telling the truth about how much fun it was and that they would be safe, but they weren't convicted to the point that they would risk jumping in. The "What if's" held them back—What if my mom doesn't catch me? What if it is not as great as it looks? What if I get cold? What if I have to go to the bathroom once I get in the water? The unknown answers, the lack of knowledge held them confined on the side.

When God asks us to take "the plunge" of faith, we are like those frozen bodies on the side of the pool. We want to jump. We believe what He tells us, and yet our minds are flooded with "What ifs"—

What if I have to change? What if I have to give up things I like? What if my friends make fun of me? What if it is not as great as He promises it will be? We squash our chances of experiencing the joy of the water, the things we hope for because we won't take the leap of faith.

But that is what faith is. It is jumping in when there is no proof of what is to come. True, the more knowledge we have, the more our faith is increased, but true faith is believing in something that is uncertain. It is not until we take that leap of faith that we will know the freedom and the joy that God has coaxed us to. When He calls us to do something and we hesitate, we are the ones who miss out on the blessings. And yet, just like our children, no amount of coaxing from Him works. We want proof. We want proof that obedience to Him is better than standing all alone on the side of the pool. Is God calling you to take a leap of faith in any area of your life? No one else can take it for you. You must learn for yourself that what He says will happen will indeed happen. Just jump. He will always be there to catch you.

Take Care of Your Things

For everyone who has will be given more, and he will have an abundance. Whoever does not have, even what he has will be taken from him.
Matthew 25: 29

Have you ever . . . gotten upset at your child for not taking care of his belongings? It could be a problem with leaving a bike in the yard allowing it to rust, or dropping expensive clothes on the floor throughout the house, or simply leaving games of a thousand pieces strewn about so that they can never be played with again. It doesn't seem to matter what the cost, children just have little regard for their possessions.

But how much do we really care for our possessions? Think of all the many gifts God has given us that we often take for granted. Obviously, the most important one is the gift of salvation. He has also given us love, family and friends, beautiful places to enjoy, and opportunities to serve. Are we being good stewards of these gifts? Do we take His love and give it to others, especially our closest family and friends? How much do we appreciate His beautiful creation in contrast to valuing material possessions? It is written, "For everyone who has will be given more." Is God pleased enough with our stewardship of His gifts to excitedly give us more?

When giving gifts to our kids, it doesn't matter if we give them a $100 bike or a five dollar ball, we expect them to take care of it. We expect them to appreciate its value, and we expect them to be responsible enough not to ruin it. We want them to learn that all things, regardless of their value, require care. Just the same, Jesus wants us to learn to care for each of our possessions. He does not care if one man has been given much and another man has been given little. He cares regardless of the initial gift He has given, but you must value it enough to care for it.

Good stewardship is a hard lesson to teach our children, and a harder lesson for God to teach us. We all want to jump over the part of being faithful in the little things and go straight in to the part of receiving "great and mighty things." We want to immediately have the big assignments from God without first showing that we are responsible enough to handle them. When you are frustrated with your abundance from God, whether it is in your career, your relationships, or your joy, think of your child who takes care of the things you give him. Don't you always want to give him more? Evaluate how much you are appreciating and caring for the things God has given you to this point. Would He be pleased to give you more as well, or are there areas in which you need to learn to be more responsible before He allows you to be in control of much?

Just Do Your Best

I have fought the good fight, I have finished the race, I have kept the faith.

2 Timothy 4:7

Have you ever . . . faced a sense of dread for a child who faced a great challenger in a competition? You knew the onslaught was imminent. I can think of many times when my son was playing sports when he went out on the field and his opponents were just huge! It looked like boys amongst men and I knew that there would be no way his team could ever be victorious. But, in spite of his team's appearance, all I really cared was that my son just did his best. It didn't matter if he walked off the field with a trophy, I just wanted to be sure that throughout the game he would give it his all.

Doing our best, giving it our all is all that God asks of us too. He knows that in the game of life we are facing the greatest opponent of all—Satan. Satan is the one who walks into our lives, proud as a peacock that he is going to defeat us. He comes in trying to scare us with his past victories embroidered on his shoulder. He taunts us, causing us to doubt any strength we might have had to oppose him. And yet, there is God on the sidelines, only expecting us to do our best, to fight the good fight, to finish the race.

There is a book by A.L. Williams entitled, *All You Can Do Is All You Can Do But All You Can Do Is*

Enough. I believe that that is how God wants us to look at this challenge we face when we go against Satan. He knows that Satan is a great challenger, but He wants us to just "do all that we can do." He wants us to do our best—that is all He asks.

God knows how scared we are when we face our greatest battles. He sees the torment we go through when we often fail in our attempts to overcome something. It is humiliating, hurtful, discouraging. But does He want us to throw in the towel because we don't stand in victory in every area of our lives? Of course not. The greatest challenge is not to be the victor but to simply cross the line, to finish the race. When you become discouraged over a failure you are trying so hard to overcome, remember God is proud of you for your best efforts. He understands the hill you are climbing. He will not blow the whistle and call you off the field as long as you are continuing to do your best!

When Are We Going to Get There?

Be patient, then, brothers, until the Lord's coming. See how the farmer waits for the land to yield its valuable crop and how patient he is for the autumn and spring rains. You too, be patient and stand firm, because the Lord's coming is near.

James 5:7-9

Have you ever . . . taken a long trip with your child and endured the question, "When are we going to get there?" Over and over he asks until you think you are going to go crazy. I've often thought that if I had a nickel for each time my children asked me this question I would be able to pay for my next vacation! It is truly one of the great tests of a parent's patience to listen to this question time and time again. And it is so difficult because of the difference in conception of time. As parents, we are able to comprehend the length of the journey so we are able to have patience until our arrival. But children don't conceptualize the length of time. They don't know the difference between a minute, an hour, or four hours, so the trip seems to go on and on forever without an end in sight.

That is how it is with God too. His conception of time is so different from ours. As a result I often find myself guilty of asking God the same question our kids ask us. When are we going to get there? When are we going to get to the point where we are able to live in peace? When will get to the place where we don't experience hardship, trouble and pain? When will we be able to do what we are supposed to do and not falter or fail? To me, it seems like the journey is taking forever as I plod along daily with the uncertainty of when I will finally arrive—arrive at the point I know God has destined for me.

But often road trips are like this. Sometimes the journey moves along quite quickly. The scenery is beautiful, circumstances are good, it is fun, fascinating and we are well contented along the route. But all of a sudden, we hit a bump in the road or the traffic comes to a standstill. Things become boring, hot and wearisome. Just like our kids, we don't feel like we can go on another mile without going crazy. Now the trip becomes drudgery and we can't wait to get off the road.

It is at this point where this Scripture comes in handy for us. When we are ready to jump ship, when we don't think we can endure the journey another minute, we must think about what we say as parents to our kids in the car. "We will get there when we get there!" Just like our children, we have the option to find a way to continue on in patience or we can choose to grumble and be miserable. Either way, we still have to stay on the journey until we reach our final destination. God doesn't want long delays to produce despair in our hearts. He doesn't want us to give up before we arrive at the place He has destined for us. So what will our choice be? I know that for me, even if the journey seems long, I will wait patiently to arrive at the wonderful place God has in store for me. What will your choice be? Can you be patient and stand firm, because the Lord's coming is near?

Give Me Rest

> The Lord is my shepherd, I shall not be in want, He makes me lie down in green pastures, he leads me beside quiet waters, he restores my soul.
> Psalm 23:1-3

Have you ever . . . wished your child would take a nap when you knew she was tired and cranky? Whether it was from a slumber party that went on too late, too many extracurricular activities at school or an oncoming sickness, you knew that your child's behavior was out of control, with whining and temper tantrums happening at the drop of a hat, all because of too little sleep. If only she would stop what she was doing, the hustle and bustle, and just lie down for some much needed rest, you were certain her behavior would improve. But what a struggle it is to get her to rest. Children hate to rest!

I believe we are as bad as our children, though, when it comes time for us to take a nap as well. Even though we say we crave time to relax, it is difficult for us to actually stop all that we are doing in our so-called "busy" lives and take the time that is needed to have our souls restored, to take the time to be with God. So what does this Scripture say God has to do? It says He MAKES us lay down to rest. Just like a child, when we are out of sorts and on overload, God has to come in and force us to take time to rest and re-energize. It is God who knows us better than we know ourselves and sees when we need our spiritual naps. If you have found yourself irritable, self-absorbed, complaining and unsatisfied, I will bet that if you look closely you will discover your need of a spiritual nap, your need of time alone with Him. God never pushes us, His sheep, further than we can go. He is too loving to see us bouncing into walls just to have us complete one more activity—even if it is for a good cause! If you will merely stop and take time to be alone with Him, you will find yourself more contented, more peaceful and more full of joy.

I know because I've experienced this. I can remember one time in particular when I was so tired and in need of rest, but instead I just kept on going and going. As a result, I spoke harshly, was quick-tempered and basically had a horrible attitude toward everything. Finally, I realized I couldn't go on, so I took a blanket and my Bible in my yard to take a nap. It was only about 15 minutes, but when I woke up I felt refreshed, and as I opened my Bible it fell to the 23rd Psalm. It said, "He makes me lie down in green pastures." There I was in the middle of my green pasture, and I realized it was God who had made me rest. So if you have found yourself lately in need of some spiritual rest, don't feel guilty about taking the time to get it. Your journey with Christ will go on for millions and millions of miles. If you don't take time to be restored by Him, you may never make it to the end!

Waiting With Patience and Confidence

> But if we hope for what we do not yet have, we wait for it patiently.
> Romans 8:25

Have you ever . . . had your child ask you for something and then watched him throw a temper tantrum when his request was not answered IMMEDIATELY? Often times when my kids ask me for something, I don't even have time to process their request before they are rolling all over the floor complaining that they don't have what they asked for. What ever happened to having a little patience? I'm sure you are like I am in that you are generally happy to help your children when they are in need. But often when they ask, you need a moment to think about their request, and you need the freedom to respond, "Wait just a minute." Children, however, have absolutely zero patience! And they have no idea what it is to wait just a minute.

The same could be said about our level of patience when we come to God asking our requests. We say a prayer and, BOOM, we want it answered. We want Him to give us what we want, help us when in need, tell us what to do, and we want it all NOW! We know that God, the bearer of all good gifts, knows the desires of our hearts and has promised to answer our prayers. We claimed those Scriptures, but did we forget to apply the part about waiting patiently for those promises to be answered? Can we, in all fairness, expect our children to wait just a minute on us and not be willing to do the same for God?

Often when I tell my child to wait, it is for a variety of different reasons. Sometimes I am in the middle of doing something else and must finish what I am doing before I can help. Sometimes, though, I have something better in store for him than what he wants and I want him to wait for that. And sometimes I ask him to wait because I know that waiting will produce a better character in him than having instant gratification. But always if I ask him to wait just a minute, it is with the promise that some action will be coming.

So it is with God that we are to wait expectantly, with patience and confidence because He has promised us a divine future. He has promised us that we will have an abundant life both now and in the life to come. We can be assured that when He speaks to our hearts and tells us to wait, something will be coming. Just as with a child, that minute may seem forever, but to God it is really no time at all. If there is something you are hoping for—a renewed relationship, the maturing of a child, maybe just a little sleep—be assured that God is our hope. He will come to bless, to restore, to fulfill, but we must wait just a minute while He processes our requests and handles our needs.

Peace and Quiet

Be still, and know that I am God.

Psalm 46:10

Have you ever . . . realized how much noise is involved with raising kids and running a home? The noise of kids yelling, televisions blaring, dishwashers and washing machines constantly humming all create a continual buzzing in our ears that we become so accustomed to, we often don't even notice they are there. The endless array of sounds drowns out our peace throughout the day and runs our batteries down so at the end of the day we have no calm or peace left in us—peace that God intended us to have not only at the beginning of each day, but at the end of each day as well.

In contrast to that, have you ever noticed the calm when all settles down at the end of the day? The kids go down for bed. The T.V. volume turns down to a bearable level. The machines stop their monotonous humming and roaring and churning and you can sink into a comfortable chair for a moment of relaxation. For me, it is as if a big wave of relief has come over me—a wave that I wasn't even aware that I needed! A sigh that causes me to wonder about all the confusion in our lives.

Did God create us to have such confusion in our lives? No! He created us to be at peace, to be able to have moments of being quiet and still so that we could be in oneness with Him. It is Satan who fills our lives with so much noise. It is Satan who says to do so much that it is impossible to have peace and quiet time with God. We get so busy and so accustomed to our day-to-day activities that we don't even notice the atmosphere of chaos that we have created around us. As we try to grind more and more out of our lives, it seems normal to be in such a frenzy. But it is only when we turn off the automatic button that runs our lives and become still that we are truly able to restore a sense of peace, because it is then that we can come to know, or as the Amplified Bible says, to recognize and to understand God.

When we become still long enough, God is able to restore us from the things in our lives that leave us feeling as if the walls are caving in on us. In our stillness He reveals Himself so that we rest in Him with all our cares, like sinking into a big easy chair. Then we fill ourselves up so that we can make it to the end of each day in peace. Of course, it is unrealistic to think we can quiet these noises from our lives completely, but we can choose to make quietness a more regular part of our lives. We can turn off the rattles and bangs and tune into God more regularly. It is our only way to keep our sanity in the midst of all the noise. So the next time you hear your dishwasher turn off and all becomes quiet, remember that God wants you to be still with Him. Give Him thanks that He handles the noise and confusion, that He will make sense of it all and be restored in the mere fact that He is God.

Super Turbo Zeo Megazord

> On his robe and on his thigh he has this name written: "KING OF KINGS AND LORD OF LORDS."
>
> Revelation 19:16

Have you ever . . . had a child interested in super heroes? It doesn't matter which one it is: Batman, Superman, Ninja Turtles, Power Rangers. They are all characters designed to show the supreme powers of the super strong good guys fighting the evil powers of the strong, but never quite as strong bad guys.

During the period that my children have grown up, the Power Rangers have been the popular strong men (and women) of the day and we have fallen heavily into the hands of the marketing strategists that have developed this series. With each new season, the strategists create bigger, stronger, more powerful weapons and vehicles with which to fight the bad guys (all of which we had to buy, of course). Their first source of power came from the Megazord, then it became the Zeo Megazord, then the Super Zeo Megazord. Finally it was the Super Turbo Zeo Megazord. Just by the name, I was convinced that this was something superduper strong to be reckoned with. The bad guys would ever be able to defeat that!

But that is the whole point of playing with super heroes. The bad guy is never supposed to win. The super hero always defeats the bad guy. He always saves the day. He is the knight in shining armor who swoops down to rescue those in trouble from the villains. That is why all the children want to be the super hero and few ever want to be the bad guy. They all want to be the one to save the day, the one who will always be the winner, the one who can overcome any situation that comes his way. The good guy never fails. No one can ever outsmart, out-force, out-maneuver the good guy.

The idea of super heroes is not limited to pretend play. We all want a Super Turbo Zeo Megazord. We all want to believe, to hope in someone who will come and rescue us from the dark forces of evil. We all want to believe that the good guy is stronger and more powerful than the bad guy. We all want good to triumph over evil. We want the knight in shining armor, the James Bond, the Super Turbo Zeo Megazord, the KING OF KINGS AND LORD OF LORDS.

And that is exactly what we find in this Scripture. We find the ultimate super hero of the world. We find the One who, no matter what predicament we find ourselves in, will save us from it. We find the One, who when we think all is doomed, comes in with one more "secret weapon" to save us from our enemy. We find the One who, just by the power of His name, KING OF KINGS AND LORD OF LORDS demonstrates there is no force that He will not be able to reckon with. Just as we know that the super hero always prevails because it is written in the script, we also know of God's victory because it is written in His script, the Bible. I urge you to put your trust in Him as the One who will save you from your fears and doubts, as the One whose victory is certain, as the One who will absolutely prevail. When you are in need of victory, whatever it may be, call on the KING OF KINGS AND LORD OF LORDS to swing into your predicament and sweep you off your feet!

Quitters Never Win

> *The end of a matter is*
> *better than its beginning.*
> *Ecclesiastes 7:8*

Have you ever . . . had your child gear up for a new activity full of excitement and total commitment, only to watch her interest fade within weeks? My children have signed up for karate, soccer, T-ball and basketball. They've taken art classes and camps which they begged to do because they all looked like so much fun! Their friends were doing it. They had visions of being star athletes, but as the weeks rolled by and the thrill wore off they wanted to quit. They began to see what making a commitment really looks and feels like, and it was then they realized that maybe their activity was not really what they wanted to do after all.

It is so easy to get excited about something new. I know because I am constantly doing this! I will buy three new books when I have four unopened at home. I'll sign up for a volunteer project when I am still complaining about the one I am currently involved in that I don't have time for. I will start a new project around the house when I still have two rooms yet to be finished. New activities always seem to come along where we jump on the band wagon with great visions of our involvement and our successes. But slowly, the excitement disappears as we realize the responsibility we have made in our commitments. It's always easier to start something than it is to finish.

It is this actuality of following through to the end though, when the going gets tough, that shapes us into better beings. When the thrill of new faces, new places and new challenges wears off and we still continue on, the making of a winner begins, no matter what the goal may be. It is where we start to separate the men from the boys so to speak. It is the time when those who are not fully committed to the goal will lose interest and go seek yet again something new.

But winners are made through perseverance. The ones who make it to the end are the true champions. Those are your success stories, your successful athletes, business people, people of real character. They are the ones who know that anyone can start something new, but to finish is the real achievement. The end of the thing is where the real pride, the real joy and the real victory take place. It is where you can turn around and see behind you a mountain of victory—a mountain of true character.

It's time to evaluate where you are in your pursuits. Are there things you need to finish? God tells us the end of a matter is better than its beginning. As you reflect on the joy you had in the beginning, believe in His promise that when you finish it will be that much sweeter—Just Finish!

Coach

"No temptation has seized you except what is common to man. And God is faithful; he will not let you be tempted beyond what you can bear. But when you are tempted, he will also provide a way out so that you can stand up under it."

1 Corinthians 10:13

Have you ever . . . had someone in your child's life that placed very high demands on him? It could be a teacher or a coach, someone who placed rigid and hard work ethics on him but consequently pushed him to soaring new heights. And they did it all by an unrelenting belief that your child could go the extra mile.

My husband is this "coach" for my kids. Although we both believe in the capabilities of our children, he is the one who can hold his ground when the going gets tough. I am the mother hen who wants to let them back off from pushing themselves too hard. But he is the one who has the confidence to always push them a little bit beyond their limits. He is the one who is always saying, "Come on you can do more. Just five more. You can do it." And I am always the one who is surprised to see that they can actually do it. He is the one who is tough on them, but he is also the one with the most faith in them!

Have you ever yearned for someone like that in your life, someone who would believe in you in everything you did, someone who would push you to new heights, encouraging you all along the way? Did you know that each of us does have that someone? It is God. He is our Coach, the One who always pushes us to go that extra mile, to set our goals higher, to strengthen our spiritual muscles. It is God who believes in us that we can endure more than what we ourselves believe we can endure.

And it is never so prevalent that God is our encouraging Coach as when we are faced with temptation. Often I feel that when I am tempted, God is discouraged with me because I so often give in. But this Scripture teaches us that God is not discouraged. He understands that "temptation is common to man." He knows the struggle to overcome, and yet He believes in our abilities that we can overcome. God doesn't convict us of our sins to make us feel bad about ourselves, but to help us be stronger. In essence, He is saying, "I know this is a temptation. But I also have faith in you that you can overcome. So let's start working on it. Others before you have made it and you can too!" God is our greatest fan club, our greatest support when it comes to believing in our strength. He allows the temptation to come into our lives so that together we can detect any imperfections in our character. We can detect those areas that need to be strengthened, that need a little practice. But all along, we can be assured that when we truly cannot go another minute, He will call "time." He better than any one knows when enough is enough.

Sticks and Stones

"The one who is in you is greater than the one who is in the world."
1 John 4:4

Have you ever . . . heard your child say to someone, "Sticks and stones may break my bones but words will never harm me?" I know personally, as a child, I said this many, many times! It is a defense mechanism to ward off anyone who attempts to tear us down with cruel words. It is a way to convince both the teaser and ourselves that whatever they are saying about us is not true. As soon as we say, "Sticks and stones may break my bones but words will never harm me," we are proclaiming, "You may say untrue things about me but I will not let it tear me down." But as much as we repeat "Sticks and stones," often it is difficult not to let these unkind words affect us. Eventually, if heard often enough, they can begin to take their root.

That is why it is so important for us to know ourselves. Because Satan, that cruel, taunting bully, is always teasing and threatening us with words that can tear us down. He loves to come in and whisper in our ears that we are no good, that we will never be able to overpower him, that we are making fools of ourselves even trying to walk righteous lives. But this is what I love about "Sticks and stones." When the devil tries to hurt us by mere words, we have the ability to brush him off. We have the ability to not be affected by his words because we know the truth about ourselves. We know that we are good, that we will overcome, that God loves it when we make our best efforts at walking righteously. And we know all this because God, who is in us, who is in our hearts, tells us so. His truth allows us to not be threatened by Satan's lies. Satan will always be a teaser and a taunter. He will always try to get us to believe his stinking lies. But we are assured that the truth of God, who is in us, is greater than the lies of Satan, who is in the world.

Whenever my kids complain that someone is teasing them, I tell them not to pay any attention to that person. They know that what the other person is saying is not true, so I tell them not to listen to the teaser. That is the same thing we should be doing to the devil. We know that what he is saying is not true, so why are we even listening? Why are we letting his false words harm and tear us down? The next time he comes in to bully you with words that make you feel bad about yourself, pay no attention to him. Rather, believe the truth about yourself promised by the One who is within you. Tell the devil, "Sticks and stones may break my bones but words will never harm me."

Winning Ugly

> *To him who overcomes, I will give the right to sit with me on my throne.*
> *Revelation 3:21*
> *He who overcomes will inherit all this, and I will be his God and he will be my son.*
> *Revelation 21:7*

Have you ever . . . had a child experience success in something knowing he had not actually deserved it? I have seen this happen many times in my child's life. Whether at a sporting event he won without playing his best, or passing a school test without studying, my child had mysteriously pulled through at the last minute to proclaim victory. It wasn't deserved and it wasn't pretty. In my days of playing tennis we used to call this "Winning Ugly"

What is "Winning Ugly"? It simply means that even though you do not do your best, you do well enough to succeed. You become a winner not because you don't make mistakes, but because you don't give up. And you don't give up because you know that in spite of your faults, in spite of your goofs, there is a prize waiting for the one who hangs on to the end. We've all seen it a million times in athletic competitions. An athlete may be on his way to imminent defeat but he hangs on, point by point, until he comes up, to everyone's surprise, victorious. Because of his ability to persevere, to set his mind on the prize, he gives everything he has to reach the goal.

Have you ever felt like your life is like that too,

that when you get to heaven, the angels will be congratulating you on an "Ugly Win"? I know I do. I look at the way I make mistake after mistake in my challenge to be a good Christian. I think about how God and everyone in heaven must cringe and murmur each time I fall into temptation: "Oh, she's fallen again. Will she be able to pick herself up?" And yet because of the prize, because of the inheritance promised in these verses, I continue to scrape my way back to stay in the fight. What I am doing is often not pretty. But the desire is strong enough to hang on to the end.

In these verses, Christ doesn't tell us we have to be perfect to get the crown. All we have to do is to finish, to overcome the hurdles along our way. So often we can be stopped dead in our tracks and defeated because we accept nothing less than perfection. If things do not go perfectly, we want to throw in the towel. But think for a moment how disappointed you would be if your child quit something, all because he had made a mistake. I want to see him face the challenge and overcome it.

And so it is with God. He is not judging winners on perfection. He is looking for those who can overcome. For He promises that those who "overcome" will sit with him on his throne and inherit His kingdom. So lighten up on yourself in the face of your failures and keep on pursuing your goal of Christ. Remember, an ugly win is still better than a pretty loss. I'd rather be victorious in Christ with a few battle scars of failure than to lose His presence in my life because I felt that if I couldn't do it perfectly, I wouldn't do anything at all.

Hurry Up! Wait! Come Back Here!

You will hear a voice behind you saying, "This is the way. Follow it, whether it turns to the right or to the left."
Isaiah 30:21

I will instruct you and teach you in the way you should go; I will counsel you and watch over you.
Psalm 32:8

Have you ever . . . tried to move a bunch of kids through a crowded mall? I get tickled at the thought of how frustrating it is. You get out of the car, holding hands, everyone is together and you are in control. Then, boom, as soon as you enter the mall, everyone goes askew. The kids are dragging behind looking at store windows, or they are running around wild chasing one another. Or, even worse, they are simply running away where you can't find them. What was once such a controlled atmosphere, with everyone in close connection, has become chaos as your clan has entered the mall and scattered, what with so many distractions and amusements.

I am usually a nervous wreck by the time I leave a shopping mall with my kids. Between the "I Wants" they have gotten from all of the stuff they have seen, to the fear of them running away where I can't find them, I am at my wits' end from giving them directions on how to behave and where to go so that we all stay together. It seems that the whole excursion is a lecture in "Hurry Up! Wait! Come Back Here!" In order to keep my children safe, to keep them from getting into trouble, to keep them from wandering off, I have spent every minute giving them directions—and as you know, that can be exhausting!

After shopping trips like this, though, I wonder how exhausting it must be for God to keep us so close to Him. Think for a minute about how many distractions are in our way that keep us from being in close connection with Him. We are distracted by the things we want and don't have. We are distracted by what everyone around us is doing and wearing and saying. We are distracted by the events taking place in our lives. But more just than being distracted, we become handfuls as we wander away and hide from Him. We think we know what we are doing when we walk off on our own, unaware of the real dangers lurking nearby. Because of this, we need that constant voice telling us to "Hurry Up! Wait! Come Back Here!" We need God's voice telling us, "This is the way. Follow it."

God is continually giving us directions on where to go in our lives. But often we just don't want to listen. We want to look at what we want and behave the way we like. But just as we are the source of wisdom and protection for our children, so is God for us. He tells us where to go and He gives us those instructions so He can keep us safe. The next time you find yourself unsure of what you should be doing or where you should be going, remember to listen for God's counsel. You wouldn't leave your child lost in the mall anymore than He would leave you when you are lost. The instruction is always there; you just have to listen out for which direction to take.

Do-Over

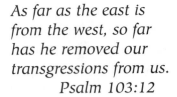

> As far as the east is
> from the west, so far
> has he removed our
> transgressions from us.
> Psalm 103:12

Have you ever . . . heard of the rule "Do-Over" in the midst of a child's game? I first heard about it in Billy Crystal's movie "City Slickers," when three men were reminiscing over their childhood games. The point of the rule was that when you were playing a game and something happened not to your liking, you would shout "Do Over" and then you would get to Do Over whatever it is you were doing!

Ever since I heard that, I have wished that we could have "Do-Overs" in the game of life. Wouldn't it be great if every time we goofed we could just shout "Do-Over" and then we could do over whatever it was we were doing! Well, guess what? In God's eyes, "Do-Overs" are possible. They are possible in every aspect of life. In fact, they are the norm for every minute, every hour or every day that we fail. Each time we mess up we get to come to God and ask Him for a "Do-Over." All we must do is say we are sorry, acknowledge that we know what we did was wrong, ask Him for His forgiveness, and God says "O.K.., you are forgiven. Try it again." And that is the end of the matter. He completely forgets about our goofs as if they had never even happened. The Bible says that "as far as the east is from the west" will He forget our mistakes and allow us to begin anew.

There is nothing that you can't do over. No mistake too big. No sin too great to be forgiven. Murder. Rape. Abuse. They are "Do-Overs". Unkind words, failed marriages, neglected loved ones, screaming at your kids, lying to a friend. They are "Do-Overs". All of them are "Do-Overs!" That is what is so beautiful about God. He is the God of new beginnings. He is the Master of new dreams and hopes. He is the King of understanding our fallen nature. He is the God of love and His love for us is too great to allow unforgiveness to separate us from Him. He can't live without His children anymore than we can live without Him. So I encourage you to always come to God for a "Do-Over." Ask for His forgiveness so that you may have your new beginning, no matter what it is you have done or how many times you have done it! He will forgive. He will forget. He will give you a fresh start to do it over again.

The Cycles of Life

What has been will be again, what has been done will be done again; there is nothing new under the sun.

Ecclesiastes 1:9

Have you ever . . . laughed at the thought of how differently we raise our first child versus our last? The first child must have his pacifier washed each time he takes it out of his mouth, but the last can practically lick the dog and no one flinches. The first one can't be out of your sight until he is 20, but the last one can go almost to the mailbox by himself at age two. The first child has a curfew of midnight even after college, but the last child will never even know what a curfew is. The poor first child receives the brunt of inexperienced parents who are overprotective and worrisome. But by the time the baby comes along, there is not a thing he can do to shock his parents.

Unfortunately, as parents we have to learn by trial and error what will hurt our children and what really won't. At the same time, we also learn that they do really survive! As time passes by, we come to see that our children's lives happen in cycles. What happens for the first child will usually come to pass for the other ones as well, and we are then that much more prepared to handle things.

In this passage from Ecclesiastes, Solomon states that "what has been will be again, what has been done will be done again; there is nothing new under the sun." What is inferred here is that things come in cycles. There are no new things, just those that come back around again. In other words, God has seen it all! There is nothing we can do to surprise Him. He has seen His children, generation after generation, going through the same stages. He knows what will be coming with each new season of our lives, just as we eventually know what will be coming with each of our subsequent children.

I've always felt this is a great lesson for those (myself included) who are afraid of approaching God for the forgiveness of certain sins. No matter how horrible your sin is, no matter how hard you try, you can't shock God! From generation to generation, God has seen the same sins over and over, and yet He still loves us. He still forgives us. He still yearns for us to come back to Him. You may think from time to time that you are too embarrassed to bring something before God for forgiveness. Yet Solomon, the wisest man ever, tells us that whatever is has already been. God has raised children from the beginning of creation and He has seen it all! Do you think there is a chance He didn't forgive the ones before you? Absolutely not! He forgave them just as He will forgive us.

Who's the Boss?

Then the Lord answered Job out of the storm. He said: "Where were you when I laid the earth's foundation? Tell me, if you understand."
Job 38:1, 4

Have you ever . . . had your child get a little full of herself and forget who was the boss in your home? Gone are the "please" and "thank you," "may I" and "will you." Instead you have, "Mom, get this!" "Mom, I need you to do something!" "Mom, do it now." In other words they start resorting to, "Give me! Do for me! And hurry it up!" I always seem to tolerate this behavior with my kids until I catch on to what is happening, and then I intervene to remind them just who the boss around our home really is.

I know we all fall into this trap. We get so used to things that others do for us that we begin to expect them to do these things rather than being thankful that they've been done in the first place. We put on an air of "it's my right" rather than an air of thanksgiving. It is what happened to Job when he began to question God about when He was going to respond, and it is what happens to us when we demand God help us— or else! I can just see Job stomping his foot, barking orders at God to answer him. Just like our children stomp their foot, put their little hands on their hips and whip out a disrespectful comment to us, so we do to God. We forget Who the boss is! We forget who is running the show. We forget who is to respond to whom. We act as if God owed us something. We act as if our demands and our needs and wishes take priority over His.

As we see here, though, it is a harsh wake up call to be reminded by God that He is really the One in control over our lives. It is a harsh reality to have Him tell us we are stepping out of line when we talk to Him. Because we have been blessed with the ability to go directly to God without any mediums, we often do so with a bold and egotistical nature as if we expect Him to do everything for us we wish. Because His nature is to be so loving and compassionate with us, we often forget His right to command respect, reverence and fear. Can you ever think of a time when maybe you have done this? Have you ever been in a predicament that you felt was undeserved—whether a divorce, financial troubles, difficult children, failing health, whatever—and responded by treating God like He just wasn't doing His job? Have you ever stomped your foot and said, "Answer me now or else!"? If the answer is yes, remember to come before God with a humbled heart. Don't be guilty of being, as my kids would say, a "sassy boots" to God. Remember, He is the One who laid the foundations of the earth and He is the One who can do to you whatever it is He pleases! He is the Boss!

The Repetition of a Good Book

> "Oh, how I love your law! I meditate on it all day long."
> Psalm 119:97
> "Blessed is the man ... whose delight is in the law of the Lord, and on his law he meditates day and night."
> Psalm 1:1-2

Have you ever... had a child ask you to read a particular book several times in a row? When my children find a book that they really love, they will sometimes ask me to read it four or five times in one sitting. I am no sooner reading "The End" than they are screaming, "Read it again, Mommy. Read it again!" In spite of the fact that I am usually ready to move on to another book, they just love hearing the same stories over and over and over.

What is it about listening to the same story time and time again? It's the familiarity and comfort that comes from that familiarity. It's the way we can unfold more about the story and the characters each time a book is read. It's the ability to see something new jump from the pages each time we read it. It's the ability to really understand the story and let it live in our hearts and become a part of us.

Often as adults though, we read a book one time and toss it aside, believing we have fully grasped its concept. We find it a burden, a waste of time to read the same book over and over rather than finding a passion in it as children do. And there is no book more in need of reading that we are quick to toss aside than the Bible. Foolishly, we think, "It is so big. It's so boring. No one can understand it, so why waste our time." Few people have found the joy in simply reading their Bibles as God intended! One of my favorite preachers, Wiley Jackson, once spoke about how people used to just sit and read their Bibles. They didn't analyze every word, they didn't get bogged down in the lists, they just read. They let it sink into their hearts and come alive. From beginning to end, they let the whole counsel of God be embedded in their hearts as they simply read through the Bible.

Repetition is the key to understanding the Bible. As we read, mysteriously God reveals himself to us. When I became a Christian, I had never even read through the Bible once. I didn't even know how you did it. Was I supposed to start with Genesis and read to the end or was there another method? I had no idea, and as I read it was confusing. But as I faithfully read every day, all of a sudden it began to make sense. All I had to do was my part, which was to read, and God did the rest. He made the stories, the characters, the meaning of His words completely come alive! The more it came alive, the more it changed every part of my life. The repetition of this Good Book is the key to coming to love it. We are to "meditate on it all day long." So don't fear your Bible. Pick it up as a child does his or her favorite book and read it over and over and over. I promise the more you do, the more it will become your favorite book to read, the more you will understand and the more it will positively change your life!

Searching for Answers

Have you ever . . . had your child try to get you to give him an answer to a problem he was working on? I can hear my kids saying, "Mom what's the answer to 3 times 6?" Or, "Mom I left my book bag at school, what should I do?" Rather than spending any time themselves trying to find a solution, they have come looking for quick and easy answers. At first these requests seem harmless. What we could answer for them in an instant would require a great amount of time for them to discover on their own. But it is important to stop, to refrain from responding, because in giving them the answers we rob them of the opportunity to discover answers for themselves.

I have found that we are often guilty of doing this to God. We have a problem and instantly we want Him to give us the answer. "If only He would just tell me what I'm doing wrong, then I could change," is our thought process. But in the long run, does that really help us? Certainly we all know God has all of the answers. He could always tell us where we are going astray. But often we have to go through those confusing valleys so that we can unwrap the mysteries ourselves. God is always there to guide us, but He is careful not to give away answers too quickly. In doing so He lets these new insights become ingrained in our being.

What do I mean? Well, think about a problem you've been facing lately, a situation where you want some clear-cut answers. Have you asked God to just fix the situation, to resolve your problem, to get you out of this mess? In doing so, you may be denying yourself of truly coming to understand the solution and let it make an impact on your life. If God gives us answers with no discovery on our part, these answers are mere Band-Aids over our wounds. They do not become a part of us as they do when we are the ones responsible for doing the searching.

The Bible tells us to seek God. It promises that if we seek God, we will find Him. In other words, we have to do the searching. We must search deep and wide to find Him, and then we will find the answers to all of our problems. He is not going to just reveal Himself and the answers to questions that we face because we want to hurry up and get through our problems, because there will always be another problem just around the corner. No, He is teaching us to answer our problems through discovering the One who knows it all. So when you find yourself confused, frustrated and yearning for answers, search for God. You will find your answers in Him, not on the silver platter He could give you.

But Why?

"*If any of you lacks wisdom, let him ask of God, who gives to all liberally and without reproach, and it will be given to him.*"
James 1:5

Have you ever . . . gotten caught up in the "But Why" game with your child? That's the one where she asks you a question, you answer it and they say "But Why?" You then give another answer and again she says, "But why?" One morning my three year old asked me why there was bird poo all over our car. I said because birds don't use the potty like we do but just poo wherever, and that wherever happened to be on our car. He said, "But why?" I said the typical, "Well, that's how God made them." He of course said again, "But why?" And along the scenario went.

I find most often when kids play the "But Why" game it is not just to drive poor parents crazy. It is done from a real sense of wanting to understand what is going on around them. The hard part though is that for most of the questions they ask, they really are not capable of understanding the answers. As parents, we want to answer them. We make attempts at giving them simplified answers that will fit into the context of their scope of knowledge. But we usually fall short of the mark because their realm of understanding is just too limited at this point.

The day I went through the frustration of trying to explain the bird poo on our car, I started to think about how often we play the "But Why" game with God. We ask Him so many questions, and we are really incapable of understanding the answers. "But why do I have to do that? But why can't I have this? But why am I hurting? But why did this happen to me?" The questions are endless. We think we know so much. We have our questions laid out before Him ready for the answers, and He looks at us, wanting to answer, knowing we don't have a clue!

The good news though is that little by little, we mature to the point where we are capable of understanding His answers. Just as our children mature in their understanding of the things of the world, we mature in our understanding of the things of God. But first we have to trust that, for now, what He says to be true is true.

The "But Why" game is most often finished with the words "Just Because!" When we come to the point as parents that we realize there is no satisfactory answer our children can understand, we use the parental authority "Just Because!" and that is the end of the discussion. In the same way, we must allow God to have that final authority in our "But Why" game. If you find that lately you have been asking Him question after question, trust that He hears and desires to answer you. Be hopeful that as you mature, God will answer all of your questions.

If You Don't Use It, You Lose It

> My son, pay attention to what I say; listen closely to my words. Do not let them out of your sight, keep them within your heart.
>
> Proverbs 4:20-21

Have you ever . . . watched a child read a book by memory? My children as preschoolers had favorite books that I would read over and over to them. After hearing the stories enough times, they would then be able to read the books themselves by memory. Just by looking at the pictures they would recall the words to the story and thus "read" the story themselves.

One day, I noticed something interesting. One of my children picked up his favorite book, Stanley, and began to "read" it, only this time he couldn't retell any of the story correctly. The reason was that he had not read Stanley in a long time and had forgotten the words. Even though he had once been able to retell the story by heart, he was now making things up and losing the context.

I started thinking about how we do that with the Bible. We read through the Bible one time and think we have the whole context of it. Or we spend years studying it in school only to drop it when we graduate believing, "I know all there is to know about that." But just like children reading by memory, "If you don't use it, you lose it!"

The other day I found myself guilty of this as I went to study a particular section of the Old Testament. I had not read the story in a long time and I had completely forgotten it. I was so surprised at all of the valuable information that I had completely forgotten. What surprised me even more was the realization of how easy it is for Satan to rob us of our memory of God's Word. He wants us to put the Bible away forever so we will never have any strength to oppose him when he attacks. But God has given us the Bible and desires for us to put it in our hearts every day so that when Satan comes, we have the guidance and strength to face the daily issues of our lives.

The day my son tried to read his book from memorization, I saw that he had twisted the words around so that the story no longer made sense. That is what we are guilty of doing when we do not listen closely to God's Word. We twist the words around and lose the context so what we preach and what we believe are false. One of the most popular phrases that people believe is in the Bible is "God helps those who help themselves." Well, that is not in the Bible. It is a phrase coined by someone who thought they knew God and His words but had "misread" Him. So remember to never let God's words out of your sight— not ever! Read them over and over and let them penetrate deep within your heart. The more they are continually in front of you, the easier they will be to recall. But as the saying goes, "If you don't use it, you will for sure lose it!" Satan will rob you like a thief in the night.

Thanks, Mom, That Hit the Spot!

> Man does not live on bread alone, but on every word that comes from the mouth of God.
>
> Matthew 4:4

Have you ever . . . fixed a meal for your children that satisfied them perfectly, leaving them saying, "Thanks, Mom, that hit the spot!"? I must admit that those types of meals are few and far between at my house, but every now and then I can pull together a meal that is perfectly satisfying and good. Even if it was just a peanut butter and jelly sandwich that happened to be the right meal at the right time, my kids have left the table feeling "just right"—not too stuffed and not still hungry.

God's Word has the potential to leave us feeling just as satisfied as a good meal? Jesus said, "Man does not live on bread alone, but on every word that comes from the mouth of God." In saying this, He meant that there is more to sustaining our bodies than just being filled up with food. We also must have regular nourishment from the Bible. We need to grow in spirit as well as stature. We need to feed our souls as well as our bodies.

It may sound strange to some that God's Word can leave us feeling so satisfied and content, but I can recall countless times that I have read the Bible and have walked away feeling this way. One time when I was totally beating myself up and was ridden with guilt over some silly, ridiculous problem, I found myself reading 1 John 3:19, "For God is greater than our hearts, and he knows everything." At that moment I felt God sharing with me, that He was not condemning me. He was greater than my heart. He knew, He understood and He still loved me. His words had comforted and sustained me at a time when I needed to be re-energized. Another time I had a friend who called to tell me this story. She was pregnant, feeling fat and miserable with nothing to wear. She said she went to her Bible and as she opened it, it fell to Matthew 6:25. "Therefore I tell you, do not worry . . . about what you will wear." She laughed, asking if that was just coincidence or what? "No," I said. "It is God giving you the right words at the right time to feed you spiritually so that you can carry on with peace of mind." It is just like the peanut butter and jelly sandwich. It doesn't have to be elaborate, just the right thing at the right time, leaving you energized, realigned and ready to go.

One of the wonderful things I have discovered about studying our Bible is that it continually becomes more and more familiar, so that when we are in need we are able to find those verses that satisfy our hungering souls. We are able to fill ourselves up on "food" that will carry us away from the draining path where we are wandering. So whenever you need a peanut butter and jelly sandwich or some meat and potatoes to fill you up, dust off the Bible and have a scrumptiously satisfying meal! Let the Bible be the nourishment that your soul needs.

Pick Me!

Then I heard the Voice of the Lord saying, "Whom shall I send? And who will go for us?" And I said, "Here am I. Send me!"
Isaiah 6:8

It is not good to have zeal without knowledge.
Proverbs 19:2

Have you ever . . . been in a classroom full of kids who were given an opportunity to answer a question? Immediately, all the hands fly up and squeals of, "Oh me. Me. Pick me," begin to echo throughout the room. Whenever I have gone to my children's classes at school and have had the opportunity to talk to their friends and ask them questions, I have always found it funny to watch their excitement in wanting to answer a question. It never mattered if they actually knew the answer to the question or not. They just automatically threw their hands in the air. But as soon as I would pick one of them, the moment of truth would follow. Would they actually have an answer or not? I would watch them looking bewildered, stuttering, "Ugh. Ugh. I don't know." And in that moment would be the realization that they had leapt before taking a look.

I can't laugh at these children too hard though, because I believe it is a reality that all of us must face at one time or another. We plunge into the future without evaluating what we are getting ourselves into.

Someone asks us to help in one way or another and instantly, without thinking, we throw our hands up in the air. "Me. Oh me. Pick me. I can do it." We want to help, to "show our stuff," but how often are we standing there with zeal but little knowledge? How often have we leapt before we looked? Especially when we claim we want to be chosen for God. He calls out, "Who will help us? Who will go?" And instantly all our hands are raised. We want to serve Him. We want the big assignment. We want our answer to make us shine. But will we be able to respond when He actually calls our names?

It is not an answer to respond to lightly. When we raise our hands and say, "Yes, I'll go," it is serious and it requires much commitment. Many are those who want and desire to serve God. But few are those who really are willing to sacrifice and endure when the going gets and stays tough. You are a mother. You have endured for your child. You know the commitment it takes. When you raise your hand for God, will you go forth with the knowledge that He has made the same commitment to you? Will you go forth with the knowledge that everything you do for your child, God is doing for you? One of my favorite songs says, "I will go Lord where you lead me. I will hold your people in my arms." As you go, as you hold your children in your arms, know that God is holding you too! God bless you! You are a child of God!